I'M SURE IT'S LOVE

"In real love you want the other person's good.
In romantic love you want the other person."
~Margaret Anderson~

I

I'm Sure It's love . . .
Not because of its shining hair
Nor the skin smooth and fair
But for its character so rare

I'm Sure It's love . . .
'Cause its worth is more than Ghana's gold
Its strength far exceeds Samson's hold
Its wisdom beyond what Sol'mon told

I'm Sure It's love . . .
'Cause in the years that have gone
Despite grinding trials it has borne
Its luster of patience has brightly shone

I'm Sure It's love . . .
'Cause for each day of affection
There's ample time for reflection
About God's plans and direction

~~~~~~

II

I'm Sure It's love . . .
'Cause it gives everything
Without expecting anything
And even willing to be nothing

I'm Sure It's love . . .
For when life's storms appear
It's near to calm and cheer
To stir my faith to persevere

I'm Sure It's love . . .
'Cause when there's a mistake
My heart does not quake
For fear our relation will break

I'm Sure It's love . . .
'Cause when I give cause for it to loathe
It never forgets its sacred oath
Before the Lord between us both
~~~~~~

III

I'm Sure It's love . . .
For it knows not "mine" or "thine"
Since our lives do now entwine
And selfless giving is there to shine

I'm Sure It's love . . .
'Cause in rainy or sunny weather
We strive to grow together
Bearing fruits for each other

I'm Sure It's love . . .
'Cause when deep wounds open
The home is never broken
Heeding what God's Word has spoken

I'm Sure It's Love . . .
For when to paths of death I stray
It calls me back to God's strait way
And walks with me to His home to stay

PART II

LOVE QUOTES

7

Cynical Versus Innocent Love

"Love is a fire. But whether it is going to warm your heart or burn down your house, you can never tell."
~Joan Crawford~

Someone has said: "When the emotion is love, everyone is a poet." Lord Byron (1788-1824) was even more insightful, when he observed: "For a man to become a poet...he must be in love or miserable."

Indeed, those who have ever tasted love in their lives—whether positively or negatively—have often written about their encounters with this powerful human experience. In this chapter, we will share a few quotes from some who apparently felt cynical about love, possibly because their own experiences in love relationships—or those they have witnessed in others—may not have been entirely favorable. We will conclude by looking at what children say about love. Theirs may be termed "innocent love."

Cynical Love Quotes

"Love is like a beautiful, endless dream . . . until you wake up."—*Sarah Higgins*

"Love is not fair. Once you find it you become a slave!"—*Unknown*

"Love is like prison, once you get in, it's hard to get out. You stress, you cry, you do things you never thought you would."—*L.E. Alston*

"Love is so deep. Once you fall in it you can never get out."—*Unknown*

"Gravitation can not be held responsible for people falling in love."—*Albert Einstein*

"Love is as unproblematic as a vehicle. The only problems are the drivers, the passengers and the road."—*Franz Kafka*

"Love is like war: Easy to begin but hard to end."—*Anonymous*

"Like the measles, love is most dangerous when it comes late in life." —*Lord Byron*

"Love is grand; divorce is a hundred grand."—*Unknown*

"Do not pray to marry the one that you love, but to love the one that you marry."—*Spencer Kimball*

"Love is a state in which a man sees things most decidedly as they are not."—*Friedrich Nietzsche*

"Love is a form of insanity that makes a girl marry her boss and work for him the rest of her life without salary."—*Unknown*

"Love is giving someone the power to destroy you."—*Gretchen Wilson*

"Many a man owes his success to his first wife . . . and his second wife to his success."—*Jim Backus*

"The girl who thinks no man is good enough for her to love may be right, but more often she is left."—*Unknown*

"Love is a pain."—*David Arroyo*

"Have you ever been in love? Horrible isn't it? It makes you so vulnerable. It opens your chest and it opens up your heart and it means that someone can get inside you and mess you up. You build up all these defenses, you build up a whole suit of armor, so that nothing can hurt you, then one stupid person, no different from any other stupid person, wanders into your stupid life. . . . You give them a piece of you. They didn't ask for it. They did something dumb one day, like smile at you, and then your life isn't your own anymore. Love takes hostages. It gets inside you. It eats you out and leaves you crying in the darkness, so simple a phrase like 'maybe we should be just friends' turns into a glass splinter working its way into your heart. It hurts. Not just in the imagination. Not just in the mind. It's a soul-hurt, a real gets-inside-you-and-rips-you-apart pain. I hate love."—*Neil Gaiman*

"How come we don't always know when love begins, but we always know when it ends?"—*L.A. Story*

"Love: A temporary insanity curable by marriage or by the removal of the patient from the influences under which he incurred the disorder. . . . It is sometimes fatal, but more frequently to the physician than to the patient."—*Ambrose Bierce*

"Marriage is love. Love is blind. Therefore marriage is an institution for the blind."—*Unknown*

"Love is one long sweet dream, and marriage is the alarm clock."—*Unknown*

"Love is much like a wild rose, beautiful and calm, but willing to draw blood in its defense."— *Mark Overby*

"They say that when a man holds a woman's hand before marriage, it is love; after marriage it is self-defense."—*Unknown*

"Love is a minefield. You take a step and get blown to pieces, put yourself back together again and stupidly take another step. I guess that's human nature. It hurts so much to be alone that we'd all rather blow up than be single."—*Kate Welles*

"A man is incomplete until he is married. After that, he is finished."—*Zsa Zsa Gabor*

"To be in love is merely to be in a state of perceptual anesthesia."—*H.L. Mencken*

"To love is to suffer. To avoid suffering, one must not love. But then, one suffers from not loving. Therefore to love is to suffer, not to love is to suffer. To suffer is to suffer. To be happy is to love. To be happy then is to suffer. But suffering makes one unhappy. Therefore, to be unhappy one must love, or love to suffer, or suffer from too much happiness. I hope you're getting this down."—*Woody Allen*

"By all means marry. If you get a good wife you will become happy, and if you get a bad one you will become a philosopher."—*Socrates*

"Do you want me to tell you something really subversive? Love is everything it's cracked up to be. That's why people are so cynical about it. It really is worth fighting for, being brave for, risking everything for. And the trouble is, if you don't risk everything, you risk even more."—*Erica Jong*

Innocent Love Quotes

A group of professional people posed this question to a group of four- to eight-year-olds, *"What does love mean?"* The answers they got were broader and deeper than anyone could have imagined. See what you think:*

"When my grandmother got arthritis, she couldn't bend over and paint her toenails anymore. So my grandfather does it for her all the time, even when his hands got arthritis too. That's love."—*Rebecca*, age 8

"When someone loves you, the way they say your name is different. You know that your name is safe in their mouth."—*Billy*, age 4

"Love is when a girl puts on perfume and a boy puts on shaving cologne and they go out and smell each other."—*Karl*, age 5

"Love is when you go out to eat and give somebody most of your French fries without making them give you any of theirs."—*Chrissy*, age 6

"Love is what makes you smile when you're tired."—*Terri*, age 4

"Love is when my mommy makes coffee for my daddy and she takes a sip before giving it to him, to make sure the taste is OK."—*Danny*, age 7

"Love is what's in the room with you at Christmas if you stop opening presents and listen."—*Bobby*, age 5

"If you want to learn to love better, you should start with a friend whom you hate."—*Nikka*, age 6

"There are two kinds of love. Our love. God's love. But God makes both kinds of them."—*Jenny*, age 4

"Love is when you tell a guy you like his shirt, then he wears it every day."—*Noelle*, age 7

"Love is like a little old woman and a little old man who are still friends even after they know each other so well."—*Tommy*, age 6

"My mommy loves me more than anybody. You don't see anyone else kissing me to sleep at night."—*Clare*, age 5

"Love is when Mommy gives Daddy the best piece of chicken."—*Elaine*, age 5

"Love is when Mommy sees Daddy smelly and sweaty and still says he is handsomer than Robert Redford."—*Chris*, age 8

"Love is when your puppy licks your face even after you left him alone all day."—*Mary Ann*, age 4

"I know my older sister loves me because she gives me all her old clothes and has to go out and buy new ones."—*Lauren*, age 4

"I let my big sister pick on me because my Mom says she only picks on me because she loves me. So I pick on my baby sister because I love her."—*Bethany*, age 4

"When you love somebody, your eyelashes go up and down and little stars come out of you."—*Karen*, age 7

"Love is when Mommy sees Daddy on the toilet and she doesn't think it's gross."—*Mark*, age 6

"You really shouldn't say 'I love you' unless you mean it. But if you mean it, you should say it a lot. People forget."—*Jessica,* age 8

And the final one . . .

Author and lecturer Leo Buscaglia once talked about a contest he was asked to judge. The purpose of the contest was to find the most caring child. The winner was a four-year-old child whose next-door neighbor was an elderly gentleman who had recently lost his wife.

Upon seeing the man cry, the little boy went into the old gentleman's yard, climbed onto his lap, and just sat there. When his mother asked what he had said to the neighbor, the little boy said, "Nothing, I just helped him cry."

Maybe if we listened to our children the world would be a better place.

Some Love Quotes From the Bible

"There is no fear in love; but perfect love casteth out fear." *1 John 4:18*

"Let brotherly love continue." *Hebrews 13:1*

"Hatred stirreth up strifes: but love covereth all sins." *Proverbs 10:12*

"And this is His commandment, That we should believe on the name of His Son Jesus Christ, and love one another, as He gave us commandment." *1 John 3:23*

"These things I command you, that ye love one another." *John 15:17*

"For all the law is fulfilled in one word, even in this; Thou shalt love thy neighbor as thyself." *Galatians 5:14*

"He that loveth not, knoweth not God; for God is love." *1 John 4:8*

"My little children, let us not love in word, neither in tongue; but in deed and in truth." *I John 3:18*

"And the Lord make you to increase and abound in love one toward another, and toward all men, even as we do toward you." *1 Thessalonians 3:12*

Notes:

* I'm indebted to Ladan Lashkari for her permission to print the compilation cited here. See her online article, "'What Does Love Mean?' See "How 4-8 Year-Old Kids Describe Love." Article source: http://www.redsofts.com/articles/read/298/49522/What_Does_Love_Mean_See_How_48_YearOld_Kids_Describe_Love.html.

8

Humorous Versus Serious Love

"Love is like a spice. It can sweeten your life—however, it can spoil it too."
~Confucius~

Love is a greatly misunderstood word. It has become an elastic word that means different things to different people. Because *love* is often misused and overused, the word tends to be distorted. Its casual use has given rise to many jokes about the experience of love. At the same time, a large body of insightful statements also exists about love.

This chapter brings together a few quotes—both humorous and serious—on love.

Humorous Love Quotes

"Everyone admits that love is wonderful and necessary . . . yet, no one agrees on just what it is."—*Diane Ackerman*

"Love is the feeling you feel, which you've never felt before the feeling you now feel."—*Unknown*

"Maybe love is like luck. You have to go all the way to find it."—*Robert Mitchum*

"Love is foolish . . . but I still might try it sometime."—*Floyd*, age 9

"Love is like quicksand: the deeper you fall in it the harder it is to get out."—*Unknown*

"True love is like ghosts, which everybody talks about and few have seen." —*La Rochefoucauld*

"Love is friendship that has caught fire."—*Ann Landers*

"Love is the irresistible desire to be irresistibly desired."—*Mark Twain*

"It takes a second to notice someone,
An hour to like someone,
A day to fall in love with someone . . .
And a lifetime to forget them."—*Brittney Shea*

"Love is like a pickle; it's sweet, sour, and it has its bumps."—*Ashlie Quillen*

"Love is blind, and marriage is an eye-opener."—*Unknown*

"Three things can't be hidden: coughing, poverty, and love."—*Yiddish proverb*

"Always love your enemies—nothing annoys them so much."—*Oscar Wilde*

"Love is the capability to evoke your loved one's love."—*Chinese saying*

"Love is running into his arms, colliding with his heart, and exploding into his soul." —*Unknown*

"Love: A term which has no meaning if defined."—*John Ralston Saul*

"Love—a wildly misunderstood although highly desirable malfunction of the heart which weakens the brain, causes eyes to sparkle, cheeks to glow, blood pressure to rise, and the lips to pucker."—*Anonymous*

"Love is a madness; if thwarted it develops fast."—*Mark Twain*

"Love's nothing else than a war in which both are the winners."—*Madonna*

"Love is like π—natural, irrational, and very important."—*Lisa Hoffman*

"I recently read that love is entirely a matter of chemistry. That must be why my wife treats me like toxic waste."—*David Bissonette*

"Love is said to be blind, but I know lots of fellows in love who can see twice as much in their sweethearts as I can."—*Josh Billings*

"The first thing a girl hopes for from the garden of love is at least one carat."—*S.S. Biddle*

"Once you have loved someone, you'd do anything in the world for them . . . except love them again."—*Unknown*

"Love is the irresistible desire to be desired irresistibly."—*Louis Ginsberg*

"Real love is a pilgrimage. It happens when there is no strategy, but it is very rare because most people are strategists."—*Anita Brookner*

"What is love but that which poisons the body, clouds the mind, yet envigorates the soul."—*Adam Murphy*

Serious Love Quotes

"I'm not rushing into being in love. I'm finding fourth grade hard enough."—*Regina,* age 10

"Loving someone is giving them the power to hurt you, but trusting them not to."—*Anonymous*

"Pain reminds us we're alive. Love reminds us why."—*Unknown*

"It is better not to live than not to love."—*Henry Drummond*

"Love is a given, hatred is acquired."—*Doug Horton*

"To get divorced because love has died, is like selling your car because it's run out of gas."—*Diane Sollee*

"Ironic, isn't it, that in tennis 'love' is nothing but in life 'love' is everything!"—*Unknown*

"If you would be loved, love and be lovable."—*Benjamin Franklin*

"Don't underestimate love at first sight. Many of us might not pass a second inspection."—*Unknown*

"They do not love that do not show their love."—*William Shakespeare*

"Love is just a word till someone you meet gives it a meaning." —*Unknown*

"Love me when I least deserve it, because that's when I really need it."—*Swedish proverb*

"To love someone deeply gives you strength. Being loved by someone deeply gives you courage."—*Lao Tzu*

"Love is not something you want, it's something you give."—*Balou Faustin*

"You can't buy love, but you can pay heavily for it."—*Henny Youngman*

"Infantile love follows the principle: 'I love because I am loved.'
Mature love follows the principle: 'I am loved because I love.'
Immature love says: 'I love you because I need you.'
Mature love says: 'I need you because I love you.'"—*Erich Fromm*

"True love is neither requested nor deserved."—*Paul Yeboah*

"LOVE, the noun, is the fruit of LOVE, the verb."—*Unknown*

"We can only learn to love by loving."—*Iris Murdoch*

"I like not only to be loved, but to be told I am loved."—*George Eliot*

"True love is giving all you have to someone you know you're going to lose."—*Ray H. Wall*

"He who falls in love with himself will have no rivals."—*Benjamin Franklin*

"Love starts with a smile, grows with a kiss, and ends with a tear." —*Unknown*

"I think that of all the diseases in the world, the disease that all humankind suffers from, the disease that is most devastating to us is not AIDS, it's not gluttony, it's not cancer, it's not any of those things. It is the disease that comes about because we live in ignorance of the wealth of love that God has for us."—*Rich Mullins*

"Take away love, and our earth is a tomb."—*Robert Browning*

"Love cannot exist without an object to love."—*Unknown*

"The only measure of your worth and your deeds will be the love you leave behind when you're gone."—*Fred Small*

"Love is like quicksilver in the hand. Leave the fingers open and it stays. Clutch it, and it darts away."—*Dorothy Parker*

"Love is the master key that opens the gates of happiness."—*Oliver Wendell Holmes*

"Love does not consist in gazing at each other but in looking together in the same direction."—*Antoine de Saint-Exupéry*

"Love is friendship set to music."—*Channing Pollock*

"Love is not something you feel. It's something you do."—*David Wilkerson*

"Love is unselfishly choosing for another's highest good."—*C.S. Lewis*

"Love has nothing to do with what you are expecting to get—only with what you are expecting to give—which is everything."—*Katharine Hepburn*

"Love can be put off, never abandoned."—*Propertius Sextus*

"Do you love me because I am beautiful, or am I beautiful because you love me?"—*Anonymous*

"Love is like a violin. The music may stop now and then, but the strings remain forever."—*Anonymous*

"Age does not protect us from love, but love to some extent protects us from age."—*Anonymous*

"Love looks through a telescope; envy through a microscope."—*Josh Billings*

"True love doesn't have a happy ending: True love doesn't have an ending."—*Anonymous*

"Love is a fabric that never fades, no matter how often it is washed in the waters of adversity and grief."—*Unknown*

'Tis better to have loved and lost, than never to have loved at all."—*Alfred, Lord Tennyson*

"Love fails, only when we fail to love."—*J. Franklin*

"An ounce of love is worth a pound of knowledge."—*John Wesley*

"Love grows by giving. The love we give away is the only love we keep."—*Elbert Hubbard*

"Now I see that there is no such thing as love unreturn'd. The pay is certain, one way or another."—*Walt Whitman*

"They say love is blindness of heart; I say not to love is blindness."—*Victor Hugo*

"If you have it [love], you don't need to have anything else, and if you don't have it, it doesn't matter much what else you have."—*Sir James M. Barrie*

"Love without marriage can sometimes be very awkward for all concerned; but marriage without love simply removes that institution from the territory of the humanly admissible."—*Katherine Anne Porter*

"We don't love qualities, we love persons; sometimes by reason of their defects as well as of their qualities."—*Jacques Maritain*

"You don't marry someone you can live with - you marry the person who you cannot live without."—*Unknown*

"Love is not love until you give it away."—*Oscar Hammerstein II*

"Love cures people, both the ones who give it and the ones who receive it."—*Dr. Karl Menninger*

"The way to love anything is to realize that it might be lost."—*G.K. Chesterton*

"Love doesn't give a person what they deserve, but what they need."—*Unknown*

"True love, at its core, is a choice. A choice to care about that person who doesn't care about you. A choice to hold someone dear, no matter what they do. To forgive them for things that they never cared enough to ask you to forgive them for. To give unreservedly of yourself and expect nothing in return. Love makes you forget about the wrongs that people do to you and only think of the good. True love is strength and courage. True love leaves no room for doubts and fears."—*Benjamin Middleton*

"To love at all is to be vulnerable."—*C.S. Lewis*

"I never knew how to worship until I knew how to love."—*Henry Ward Beecher*

"Love is a tender, heavenly plant that needs constant cultivation in order to flourish."—*Ellen G. White*

Some Bible Love Quotes

"Whoever pursues godliness and unfailing love will find life, godliness, and honor."—*Proverbs 21:21*

"Hatred stirs up quarrels, but love covers all offenses."—*Proverbs 10:12*

"Disregarding another person's faults preserves love; telling about them separates close friends."—*Proverbs 17:9*

"Do not arouse or awaken love until it so desires."—*Song of Songs 2:7; 3:5; 8:4*

"My lover is mine and I am his."—*Song of Songs 2:16*

"For love is as strong as death, its jealousy unyielding as the grave. It burns like blazing fire, like a mighty flame. Many waters cannot quench love; rivers cannot wash it away."—*Song of Songs 8:6, 7*

"If one were to give all of his house for love, it would be utterly scorned."—*Song of Songs 8:7b*

9

Fake Versus True Love—Part I

"Lust is the forest fire that destroys everything in its path. Love is a torch that burns intensely and bonds two hearts."
~Unknown~

Socrates once said, "The hottest love has the coldest end." Such is the nature of infatuation or counterfeit love. Often, this kind of love leads no farther than a temporary emotional attachment, which almost always ends up in a painful breakup—whether before or after one gets married.

Sometimes the breakup begins with an innocent statement such as, "We need to talk." Then it is followed by a string of clichéd breakup lines, calculated to end a relationship "painlessly." But there is no such thing as a "painless" breakup. It always hurts when relationships end, even if it is for no other reason than the regret of wasted time, resources, emotions, and even self-dignity.

Those who want to avoid the ugly scars of any breakup should not fall for infatuation, or fake love.

This chapter brings together some well-known breakup quotes, together with valuable insight on fake love. The next chapter will continue the discussion by looking at some relevant quotes on true love.

Breakup Love Quotes

The Bible tells us that true love never fails (1 Corinthians 13:7, 8, 13). But counterfeit love always betrays the object of its initial affection, when it calls off the relationship. Breakups in fake love relationships are always necessary and should be welcomed. But they still hurt, and in some cases they cause some deep wounds and ugly scars.

Apparently to minimize the pain resulting from such failed relationships, euphemistic expressions are often employed. The irony is, sometimes those who have been blinded by infatuation do not realize that they have been abandoned!

The most well-known of the standard breakup lines are the different variations of the "It's-not-about-you" quotes: "It's not you—it's me"..."It's not you or me—it's us"..."It's not you—it's them."

Though the above lines sound innocent enough, the bottom line is, the person's "love" for you is over. In many cases, when they tell you "It's not about you—but me," it really means "It's about *you*. It's your fault, but I don't want to hurt your feelings by saying so." Regardless of the real reason, every breakup simply announces that the "love" that was once professed has come to an end.

The following are some classic breakup lines that have come to my attention. Though each of the standard lines sounds different, these diplomatic lines are all meant to say the same thing—namely, "I don't need you anymore. Goodbye!" No one need be fooled by the "nice," innocent, or pious way a breakup line is used. The bottom line is: "It's over!" Here they are:

"I have something I need to talk to you about. It's going to hurt me more than you, but . . ."

"I don't know what's wrong with me. I really like you, but I don't know what I want. This is why I don't feel comfortable continuing the relationship."

"You deserve someone much better than me."

"I really love you, but I'm not *in* love with you."

"We have the perfect love, just at the wrong time. I'm so sorry."

"Whatever feelings I had for you in the beginning, I have lost in the end."

"I moved things *too* fast between us. It was my fault."

"Actually, I think I see you more as a friend than anything else."

"You're my best friend in the world, and I love you to death . . . but you're like a sister/brother to me."

"I don't deserve you. I wish you the best in your next relationship."

"We just don't deserve each other."

"It's no one's fault."

"There just isn't any future for us."

"I have a lot of growing up to do."

"I need to be able to branch out more."

"I've got too much going on right now to be in a relationship."

"I adore you, but I've discovered I'm attracted to someone else."

"We just don't understand each other."

"I'm pregnant. It's not yours."

"I've decided to become a nun."

"I've decided to become a priest."

"I need to concentrate on my relationship with the Lord."

"Why don't you see a few new people, and I'll see a few new people; and we'll see if we still miss each other after that."

"Our relationship isn't perfect, so I don't feel we should pursue it any further."

"If we let it go and it comes back to us, then it's meant to be."

"I feel like I'm holding you back."

"There's no easy way for me to say it, but . . ."

"I respect and appreciate you too much to not be honest with you."

"We should take a break."

"I don't think this is working out."

"In order to be very sure I want to spend the next 50 years with you, I want to see other people."

"I really like you and respect you, but I need some time to pull myself together."

"What? Were we in a *relationship*? I thought we were just *friends*."

"I'm not yet ready to settle down."

"We're at different places in our lives."

"My parents insist that I can't have a relationship right now."

"I think we should see other people."

"I need to find out more about myself."

"I just can't love someone who would love someone like me."

"I'm leaving the country, and I don't know how long I'll be gone."

"I really need to focus on my studies/job right now."

"I don't know how to say this, but . . . I can't see you anymore."

"You're still my best friend, and I love you; but we need to be independent of each other—at least for now."

"I wish I loved you; I really do. I can't understand why I don't."

"I love you, but being with you is limiting your ability to meet the right person who would want to marry you."

"I know we've had some good times together and yes, you've been there for me. No, no, it's not you; it's me! I've changed."

"I mean it when I say I greatly appreciate you for helping me out when I needed it. But I think I can take it from here."

"Though it didn't work out, the time we *had* together was one of the best periods in my life."

"We can still be good friends, hang out together from time to time—even though we must each be free to see other people as well."

"I think we both know this isn't working out."

"I think one of us knows this isn't working out."

"My mum is having a problem with our relationship."

"It's not you; it's me."

"It's not me, it's you."

"My sister thinks we should break up, and I think I agree with her."

"I don't know why, but we just don't click anymore."

"Let's not take it too personally; if we are meant for each other we'll be back together again."

"Nothing has changed between us. We're still very good friends. I just want to explore my feelings for someone else, to find out how much I really love you."

"I can't be with you because I love you more than you love me."

There are also some interesting "Christian breakup quotes." Here are a few of them:

"I'm sorry, it's just not God's will."

"I've been praying a lot lately about our relationship. I think we should not rush the Lord."

"The Lord has shown me that I'm not ready, and if we continue I'll most likely hurt you."

"We're living in the last days and I want to focus my attention on the Lord's work."

"Would you happen to know another Christian that I could love with all my heart?"

"I do love you, but it's just *agape* now."

"I think we should just be prayer partners."

As mentioned earlier, though each of these standard lines sounds different, these diplomatic and even "spiritual" lines are all meant to say the same thing—namely, "I don't need you anymore. Goodbye—and good luck!" The bottom line is: "It's over!" And with that, the dream of fake love reveals itself for what it really is—a nightmare.

But it should be noted that, many of these painful breakups could have been prevented in the first place, if we had refused to fall for blind love or infatuation. Often, the warning signals have been there all along, but we failed to see them.

How can we tell when we are being fooled? In the long quotation below, my favorite devotional writer offers some insightful cautions against fake, or counterfeit love.

When Love Is Blind*

Two persons become acquainted; they are infatuated with each other, and their whole attention is absorbed. Reason is blinded, and judgment is overthrown. They will not submit to any advice or control, but insist on having their own way, regardless of consequence.

Like some epidemic, or contagion, that must run its course, is the infatuation that possesses them; and there seems to be no such thing as putting a stop to it. Perhaps there are those around them who realize that, should the parties interested be united in marriage, it could only result in life-long unhappiness. But entreaties and exhortations are given in vain. Perhaps, by such a union, the usefulness of one whom God would bless in His service will be crippled and destroyed; but reasoning and persuasion are alike unheeded.

All that can be said by men and women of experience proves ineffectual; it is powerless to change the decision to which their desires have led them. They lose interest in everything that pertains to religion. They are wholly infatuated with each other, and the duties of life are neglected, as if they were matters of little concern.

The good name of honor is sacrificed under the spell of this infatuation, and the marriage of such persons cannot be solemnized under the approval of God. They are married because passion moved them, and when the novelty of the affair is over, they will begin to realize what they have done. In six months after the vows are spoken, their sentiments toward each other have undergone a change. Each has learned in married life more of the character of the companion chosen. Each discovers imperfections that, during the blindness and folly of their former association were not apparent. The promises at the altar do not bind them together. In consequence of hasty marriages, even among the professed people of God, there are separations, divorces, and great confusion in the church.

When it is too late, they find that they have made a mistake, and have imperiled their happiness in this life and the salvation of their souls. They would not admit that any one knew anything about the matter but themselves, when if counsel had been received, they might have saved themselves years of anxiety and sorrow. But advice is only thrown away on those who are determined to have their own way. Passion carries such individuals over every barrier that reason and judgment can interpose.

Weigh every sentiment, and watch every development of character in the one with whom you think to link your life destiny. The step you are about to take is one of the most important in your life, and should not be taken hastily. While you may love, do not love blindly.

I hope you will have self-respect enough to shun this form of courtship. If you have an eye single to the glory of God, you will move with deliberate caution. You will not suffer lovesick sentimentalism to so blind your vision that you cannot discern the high claims that God has upon you as a Christian.

~~~~~
~~~~~

In the light of the above counsel, you can, perhaps, better appreciate the poems in chapter 5, especially these two:

It's Not Love . . .
When feelings dismiss common sense
The voice of conscience is nonsense
And the Moral Law is an offense

It's Not Love . . .
When your kiss it seduces to sip
Then bites and wounds your soul's lip
Scarring your life with a guilt trip.

Notes:

* Ellen G. White was a nineteenth–century Christian author, well respected for her classic works on biblical spirituality and Christian living. The quote in this section is from her *Letters to Young Lovers* (Mountain View, Calif.: Pacific Press, 1983), pp. 33–35—a compilation of her letters to young people to help them make the right choices relating to their courtship and marriage.

10

Fake Versus True Love—Part II

"Love is a fruit in season at all times, and within the reach of every hand."
~Mother Teresa~

The apostle Paul admonishes us: "Don't just pretend to love others. Really love them. Hate what is wrong. Hold tightly to what is good. Love each other with genuine affection [or brotherly love], and take delight in honoring each other" (Romans 12:9, 10, *New Living Translation*).

Paul wants us to distinguish between pure, unselfish love prompted by the Spirit of Christ, and the unmeaning, deceitful pretense that abounds in the world. In the previous chapter, we focused on counterfeit love and how it often results in some painful breakups.

The present chapter is a continuation of the previous one, highlighting the nature of true love. The selected quotes or counsels below are from the author's esteemed devotional writer. They can shield us from the painful consequences of a fake love. The selection also gives directions regarding what to look for in a prospective partner—and even offers a suggestion on when and how to break an unwise relationship!

True Love[1]

True love is a high and holy principle, altogether different in character from that love which is awakened by impulse and which suddenly dies when severely tested.

True love is not a strong, fiery, impetuous passion. On the contrary, it is calm and deep in its nature. It looks beyond mere externals and is attracted by qualities alone. It is wise and discriminating, and its devotion is real and abiding.

Love is a precious gift, which we receive from Jesus. Pure and holy affection is not a feeling, but a principle. Those who are actuated by true love are neither unreasonable nor blind.

Mildness, gentleness, forbearance, long-suffering, being not easily provoked, bearing all things, hoping all things, enduring all things—these are the fruit growing upon the precious tree of love, which is of heavenly growth. This tree, if nourished, will prove to be an evergreen. Its branches will not decay, its leaves will not wither. It is immortal, eternal, watered continually by the dews of Heaven.

Love—a Tender Plant

Love is a plant of heavenly growth, and it must be fostered and nourished. Affectionate hearts, truthful, loving words, will make happy families and exert an elevating influence upon all who come within the sphere of their influence.

While women want men of strong and noble characters, whom they can respect and love, these qualities need to be mingled with tenderness and affection, patience and forbearance. The wife should in her turn be cheerful, kind, and devoted, assimilating her taste to that of her husband as far as it is possible to do without losing her individuality. Both parties should cultivate patience and kindness, and that tender love for each other that will make married life pleasant and enjoyable.

Those who have such high ideas of the married life, whose imagination has wrought out an air-castle picture that has naught to do with life's perplexities and troubles, will find themselves sadly disappointed in the reality. When real life comes in with its troubles and cares, they are wholly unprepared to meet them. They expect in each other perfection, but find weakness and defects; for finite men and women are not faultless. Then they begin to find fault with each other, and to express their disappointment. Instead of this, they should try to help each other, and should seek practical godliness to help them to fight the battle of life valiantly.

The Power of Love

Love is power. Intellectual and moral strength are involved in this principle, and cannot be separated from it. The power of wealth has a tendency to corrupt and destroy; the power of force is strong to do hurt; but the excellence and value of pure love consist in its efficiency to do good, and to do nothing else than good.

Whatsoever is done out of pure love, be it ever so little or contemptible in the sight of men, is wholly fruitful; for God regards more with how much love one worketh than the amount he doeth.

Love is of God. The unconverted heart cannot originate nor produce this plant of heavenly growth, which lives and flourishes only where Christ reigns. . . .

Love works not for profit nor reward; yet God has ordained that great gain shall be the certain result of every labor of love. It is diffusive in its nature and quiet in its operation, yet strong and mighty in its purpose to overcome great evils. It is melting and transforming in its influence, and will take hold of the lives of the sinful and affect their hearts when every other means has proved unsuccessful.

Wherever the power of intellect, of authority, or of force is employed, and love is not manifestly present, the affections and will of those whom we seek to reach assume a defensive, repelling position, and their strength of resistance is increased.

Pure love is simple in its operations, and is distinct from any other principle of action. The love of influence and the desire for the esteem of others may produce a well-ordered life and frequently a blameless conversation. Self-respect may lead us to avoid the appearance of evil. A selfish heart may perform generous actions, acknowledge the present truth, and express humility and affection in an outward manner, yet the motives may be deceptive and impure; the actions that flow from such a heart may be destitute of the savor of life and the fruits of true holiness, being destitute of the principles of pure love.

Love should be cherished and cultivated, for its influence is divine.

Qualities to Consider in a Relationship[2]

Great care should be taken by Christian youth in the formation of friendships and in the choice of companions. Take heed, lest what you now think to be pure gold turns out to be base metal. Worldly associations tend to place obstructions in the way of your service to God, and many souls are ruined by unhappy unions, either business or matrimonial, with those who can never elevate or ennoble. Never should God's people venture upon forbidden ground. Marriage between believers and unbelievers is forbidden by God. But too often the unconverted heart follows its own desires, and marriages unsanctioned by God are formed.

Let those who are contemplating marriage weigh every sentiment and watch every development of character in the one with whom they think to unite their life destiny. Let every step toward a marriage alliance be characterized by modesty, simplicity, sincerity, and an earnest purpose to please and honor God. Marriage affects the afterlife both in this world and in the world to come. A sincere Christian will make no plans that God cannot approve.

Qualities to Be Sought in a Prospective Wife[3]

Let a young man seek one to stand by his side who is fitted to bear her share of life's burdens, one whose influence will ennoble and refine him, and who will make him happy in her love.

"A prudent wife is from the Lord." "The heart of her husband doth safely trust in her. . . . She will do him good and not evil all the days of her life." "She openeth her mouth with wisdom; and in her tongue is the law of kindness. She looketh well to the ways of her household, and eateth not the bread of idleness. Her children arise up, and call her blessed; her husband also, and he praiseth her," saying, "Many daughters have done virtuously, but thou excellest them all." He who gains such a wife "findeth a good thing, and obtaineth favor of the Lord."

Here are things which should be considered: Will the one you marry bring happiness to your home? Is [she] an economist, or will she, if married, not only use all her own earnings, but all of yours to gratify a vanity, a love of appearance? Are her principles correct in this direction? Has she anything now to depend upon? . . . I know that to the mind of a man infatuated with love and thoughts of marriage these questions will be brushed away as though they were of no consequence. But these things should be duly considered, for they have a bearing upon your future life. . . .

In your choice of a wife study her character. Will she be one who will be patient and painstaking? Or will she cease to care for your mother and father at the very time when they need a strong son to lean upon? And will she withdraw him from their society to carry out her plans and to suit her own pleasure, and leave the father and mother who, instead of gaining an affectionate daughter, will have lost a son?

Qualities to Be Sought in a Prospective Husband[4]

Before giving her hand in marriage, every woman should inquire whether he with whom she is about to unite her destiny is worthy. What has been his past record? Is his life pure? Is the love which he expresses of a noble, elevated character, or is it a mere emotional fondness? Has he the traits of character that will make her happy? Can she find true peace and joy in his affection? Will she be allowed to preserve her individuality, or must her judgment and conscience be surrendered to the control of her husband? . . . Can she honor the Saviour's claims as supreme? Will body and soul, thoughts and purposes, be preserved pure and holy? These questions have a vital bearing upon the wellbeing of every woman who enters the marriage relation.

Let the woman who desires a peaceful, happy union, who would escape future misery and sorrow, inquire before she yields her affections, Has my lover a mother? What is the stamp of her character? Does he recognize his obligations to her? Is he mindful of her wishes and happiness? If he does not respect and honor his mother, will he manifest respect and love, kindness and attention, toward his wife? When the novelty of marriage is over, will he love me still? Will he be patient with my mistakes, or will he be critical, overbearing, and dictatorial? True affection will overlook many mistakes; love will not discern them.

Let a young woman accept as a life companion only one who possesses pure, manly traits of character, one who is diligent, aspiring, and honest, one who loves and fears God.

Shun those who are irreverent. Shun one who is a lover of idleness; shun the one who is a scoffer of hallowed things. Avoid the society of one who uses profane language, or is addicted to the use of even one glass of liquor. Listen not to the proposals of a man who has no realization of his responsibility to God. The pure truth which sanctifies the soul will give you courage to cut yourself loose from the most pleasing acquaintance whom you know does not love and fear God, and knows nothing of the principles of true righteousness. We may always bear with a friend's infirmities and with his ignorance, but never with his vices. . . .

You may say, "But I have given my promise, and shall I now retract it?" I answer, If you have made a promise contrary to the Scriptures, by all means retract it without delay, and in humility before God repent of the infatuation that led you to make so rash a pledge. Far better take back such a promise, in the fear of God, than keep it, and thereby dishonor your Maker.

Let every step toward a marriage alliance be characterized by modesty, simplicity, sincerity, and an earnest purpose to please and honor God. Marriage affects the afterlife both in this world and in the world to come. A sincere Christian will make no plans that God cannot approve.

Breaking an Unwise Relationship[5]

What ought every Christian to do when brought into the trying position which tests the soundness of religious principle? With a firmness worthy of imitation he should say frankly, "I am a conscientious Christian. I believe the seventh day of the week to be the Sabbath of the Bible.[6] Our faith and principles are such that they lead in opposite directions. We cannot be happy together, for if I follow on to gain a more perfect knowledge of the will of God, I shall become more and more unlike the world. If you continue to see no loveliness in Christ, no attractions in the truth, you will love the world, which I cannot love, while I shall love the things of God, which you cannot love. You will not be happy; you will be jealous on account of the affections which I give to God; and I shall be alone in my religious belief. When your views shall change, when your heart shall respond to the claims of God, and you shall learn to love my Saviour, then our relationship may be renewed."

The believer thus makes a sacrifice for Christ which his conscience approves, and which shows that he values eternal life too highly to run the risk of losing it. He feels that it would be better to remain unmarried than to link his interest for life with one who chooses the world rather than Jesus, and who would lead away from the cross of Christ.

Notes:

1. The following selection on love was written by nineteenth-century devotional author Ellen G. White (1827–1915), whose writings spanned the work of religious contemporaries such as Charles Spurgeon and Oswald Chambers. As mentioned in chapter 9, note 1, Mrs. White is well respected for her classic works on biblical spirituality and Christian living. A compilation of her writings on the subject of love and relationships can be found in her *Letters to Young Lovers* (Nampa, ID: Pacific Press, 1983), *Messages to Young People* (Hagerstown, MD: Review and Herald, 1930) and *The Adventist Home* (Hagerstown, MD: Review and Herald, 1952). The quote cited here is from her *Letters to Young Lovers*, pp. 29-33; cf. *Adventist Home*, pp. 50-54.
2. Ellen. G. White, *Messages to Young People*, pp. 436, 435.
3. Ellen G. White, *The Adventist Home*, pp. 45, 46.
4. Ibid., pp. 47-49.
5. Ibid., pp. 67, 68.

6. Though the author's counsel was initially directed to Christians who observe the seventh day (Saturday) as the Sabbath of the Lord, the principle of being true to one's religious or biblical convictions is valid in all cases. For Sabbathkeepers such as Seventh-day Adventists and Seventh Day Baptists, the counsel by Mrs. White is particularly crucial in any meaningful relationship, since it deals with their understanding of an oft-ignored biblical truth. See Genesis 2:1-3; Exodus 20:8-11; Luke 4:16; 23:50–24:1; Acts 13:42, 44; 16:13; 17:2; 18:4; Hebrews 4:4, 9).

PART III

LOVE NOTES

11

Faces of Love

"Love is like a rumor; everyone talks about it, but no one truly knows."
~Anonymous~

One of the problems we encounter in any discussion of love is that there are many different definitions of the word. For some, the word *love* may express taste or fondness (as in "I love ice cream"), preference (as in "I love Toyota cars"), endearment or affection (as in "I love my child, wife, husband, mother, etc."), religious devotion (as in "I love Jesus"), or even sex (as in "they made love to one another").

According to Bartlett's list of quotations, there are some 2,000 different interpretations of the meaning of love by poets, philosophers, and authors. Everyone is looking for love, but we're not entirely sure what it is.

During Bible times, different words were employed for love. The variety of the meanings ranges from God's infinite lovingkindness (a reflection of His character) to the different kinds of love in human relationships. The meaning of the words for love also include human beings' attitudes toward concrete or inanimate objects, such as food, money, sex, sleep, etc. Because of space limitations, we will only look at some well-known Greek terms.[1]

Three Words for Love

During New Testament times, three words were frequently used for "love": *eros, philos,* and *agape.* Two of these are found in the New Testament—*philos* and *agape.* Let's briefly look at these three different kinds of love:

***1. Eros* Love** (from which we get our word *erotic*) is passionate love that desires the other for itself. Though the term *eros* was widely used during New Testament times, it was never used in the New Testament itself. It was the name for the god of love in Greek culture.

Eros love has to do with the physical and sensual. Unfortunately, it has developed a bad name among Christians because it is commonly associated with lust or sexual immorality. While this is true, *eros* is more than a mere sexual desire. Generally speaking, it has to do with an intense desire, ardency, or passion—or an association with the majestic, beautiful, or awesome—that stirs the human soul.

Eros is that which moves us to tears when we hear a particular type of music, when we see a sunset, or when a majestic mountain or landscape moves us to silence and awe. It is the rush of wonder, amazement, or pleasure that comes when our national soccer team scores a goal during the World Cup or, in America, when our football player scores a touchdown in the Super Bowl.

English dictionaries define *eros* as "the sum of life-preserving instincts that are manifested as impulses to gratify basic needs (as sex), as sublimated impulses motivated by the same needs, and as impulses to protect and preserve the body and mind." Or, as "the aggregate of pleasure-directed life instincts whose energy is derived from libido."

Since *eros* is understood as an "instinct" or as springing from "libido" (sexual drive), this kind of love has the capacity to be blind or without restraint. This is what happens when we are infatuated yet think we are really in love.

But it should be noted that, although *eros* love is often misunderstood and abused, in its proper context it is something beautiful. It describes that mysterious, magical, mystical, or intense feeling that we have for the people we love. It is the kind of love you see in the eyes of two people who are madly in love.

***2. Philos* Love** (from *phileo*—from which we get our words philanthropy, philosophy, Philadelphia[2]). This refers to friendly affection, closeness, deep caring, or kindness. *Philos* love is the kind of fondness we have for one another, whether friends, parents, children, or couples.

Philos love is similar to *eros* love, in that both represent a love that is the response of the human spirit to what appeals to it as pleasurable. But more generally, *philos* love refers to tender affection or fondness.

The above two kinds of love—*eros* love and *philos* love—have some things in common. They both participate in the law of cause and effect. Thus, if I'm fond of you (*philos*), you will love me back. If there's something about you that awes or wows me (*eros*), I may be drawn to love you or have a feeling for you. These two kinds of love exist because of what one person experiences with, gets from, or does with another.

Moreover, *eros* love and *philos* love are not distinctively human experiences. Animals also experience these two kinds of love (*eros* and *philos*). Like human beings, animals can be affectionate (*philos*) and can be aroused to respond in a physical way (*eros*).

Furthermore, these two kinds of love *cannot* legitimately be forced upon anyone. For example, I cannot compel you to be fond of me (*philos*) or have a feeling for me (*eros*). If I attempt to compel, it constitutes coercion or rape.[3]

Finally, *eros* love and *philos* love are *not* the love enjoined upon human beings by God's moral law—the Ten Commandments. The New Testament writers coined a completely different word to describe the love commanded by God. This third word is *agape.*

***3. Agape* Love** is a willing, selfless, and sacrificial love. It is almost exclusively used to describe God's love. As a noun, it is almost never found in Greek literature before the Christian era. *It is a noble love springing from principle.*

Although in some contexts it is sometimes used interchangeably with *phileo* (to refer to tender affection),[4] *agape* love is a totally selfless or self-sacrificing love.

The Bible describes *agape* love as follows: "Love [*agape*] is patient, love is kind. It does not envy, it does not boast, it is not proud. It is not rude, it is not self-seeking, it is not easily angered, it keeps no record of wrongs. Love does not delight in evil but rejoices with the truth. It always protects, always trusts, always hopes, always perseveres. Love never fails" (1 Corinthians 13:4-8).

Uniqueness of *Agape* Love

For love to be true love, it must spring from *agape* love. In other words, without *agape* love, the other kinds of love (*eros* and *philos*) have no true depth.

***Agape* Love Is Principled Love.** Even though the fruit of *agape* love always includes the passionate emotions of fondness, kindness, and tender affection (just as is the case in *philos* and *eros*), *agape* love does not spring from cause and effect, instinct, or libido. *Agape love is a divine principle.* It is not based on what the other person is or does. Rather, *it is an act of conscious choice (an expression of the will).*

In *agape* love, you *choose* to love the other person regardless of who they are or what they do. It is a voluntary and unconditional act of the will. It is a selfless, sacrificial giving of oneself. And because *agape* love is principled love, it can be commanded.

***Agape* Love Can Be Commanded.** At least fifty-five times in the New Testament we are commanded to love. For example, the Bible says "love your enemy," "love your neighbor as yourself," "love one another," "love your wives," etc.[5]

Because *agape* love can be commanded, God's Moral Law—the Law that reveals our love for God and man—is called the Ten *Commandments.* Though the commandments are an expression of love, they remain just that: commandments. They summarize what love is all about,[6] and set forth what God expects from us.[7]

The Ten Commandments are the very nature of love itself. This is why Jesus says: "If you love Me, keep My commandments. . . . He who has My commandments and keeps them, it is he who loves Me. And he who loves Me will be loved by My Father, and I will love him and manifest Myself to him."[8]

Again, He says: "If you keep My commandments, you will abide in My love, just as I have kept My Father's commandments and abide in His love. These things I have spoken to you, that My joy may remain in you, and that your joy may be full. This is My commandment, that you love one another as I have loved you. Greater love has no one than this, than to lay down one's life for his friends" (John 15:10-13).

Agape love is, therefore, not primarily a feeling. It is a choice. It is a responsibility. It is an action. Hence, we are commanded to love, whether or not we feel like it. It is because this kind of love is a voluntary choice that it is the basis of the Christian ethic. Loving one's enemies and doing good to them, even though they don't deserve it, is what *agape* is all about.

Though *agape* love is costly, there is a special kind of joy that comes when this kind of love is expressed—an inner joy and peace that results from doing the right thing and being in God's will.

***Agape* Love Reflects God's Character.** Without the divine principle of *agape* love, the two other kinds of love can give up on a person—when it is not in one's best interest to keep loving the other person. But *agape* love never fails. *Agape* love continues to be loving and kind, because it chooses to do so, regardless of what it will get from another person. This is a reflection of God's self-sacrificing character.

Only God has this kind of love. That's why the Bible says, "God is love" (1 John 4:8, 16). Actually, God's name can be used as a substitute for the word *love* in the love passage of 1 Corinthians 13:4-8:

> "[*God*] is patient, [*God*] is kind. [*He*] does not envy, [*He*] does not boast, [*He*] is not proud. [*He*] is not rude, [*He*] is not self-seeking, [*He*] is not easily angered, [*He*] keeps no record

of wrongs. [*God*] does not delight in evil but rejoices with the truth. [*He*] always protects, always trusts, always hopes, always perseveres. [*God*] never fails."

No other human being can perfectly fit the above description of love. Try substituting *your* name in this passage, and see how it sounds. Try the names of friends, spouse, child, parents, or anyone you hold dear. You will discover that, however loving they may be to you, they fall short of God's *agape* love.

The reason why only God's name fits perfectly is because God *is* love. The reason ours don't fit well is because too often, we do not reflect the character of God perfectly. We can experience and share this *agape* love if, and only if, we have God in our lives. Such a love is possible when we accept Jesus Christ as our Lord and Saviour.

***Agape* Love Is Evidence of True Spirituality.** Since *agape* love is principled or divine love, only those who truly know the Lord can manifest this kind of love.

The apostle John declares that "everyone who loves is born of God and knows God. He who does not love does not know God, for God is love. . . . If we love one another, God abides in us, and His love has been perfected in us. . . . We love Him because He first loved us. If someone says, 'I love God,' and hates his brother, he is a liar; for he who does not love his brother whom he has seen, how can he love God whom he has not seen? And this commandment we have from Him: that he who loves God must love his brother also" (1 John 4:7-21).

As we noted earlier, for love to be true love, it must spring from *agape* love. For without *agape* love, the other kinds of love (*eros* and *philos*) have no true depth. Thus, even though everyone can show some form of love (*philos* and *eros*), only those who know the Lord can truly love with *agape* love.

Stated differently, whenever those who don't profess belief or faith in God display genuine (*agape*) love, it is only because theirs is a reflection of God's love—whether or not the individuals involved are aware of it. Such people may be showing an *agape* love of God, even though they may not even be mindful that their love has its source in God or is a gift from God.

It should also be emphasized that although *agape* love is principled love, it brings with it the joy of pure affections and emotions that are expressed in *philos* love and *eros* love. However, *agape* love elevates these other two kinds of human emotion by anchoring them in a divine principle. In other words, where *agape* is present, there is a deep tenderness of affection (*philos*) and a quiet and beautiful display of passion (*eros*).

Human love tends to be only on the level of *philos* or *eros*. God's love is *agape*. Our love shares in the law of cause and effect. But God's *agape* love is principled and sacrificial. Only when we have God in our lives—only when we know Him (not just know *about* Him)—can we truly love Him and love other human beings. And only then can we experience the inner satisfaction or fulfillment of true love.

Notes:

1. In the Hebrew Bible (the Old Testament), a number of words were used for love. They include the following: *'ahab, 'ohab, 'hābâ*—a more general group of words used for different expressions of love—between God and human beings, among people, or people's love for things. Such expressions of love can be right or wrong, depending on context. For example, *'hābâ* describes the love of Jacob for Rachel, God's "love" for His people, and Jonathan's affection for David. It is also used with a negative connotation for "hired lovers" or prostitutes (i.e., love with illicit overtones; see Hosea 2:7; 9:12; Ezekiel 16:33, 36, 37; cf. Proverbs 7:18). This term (*'hābâ*) is frequently used in the Song of Songs. It is the term for love in several familiar verses, e.g., "His banner over me is love" (2:4); "Love is strong as death" (8:6); "Many waters cannot quench love" (8:7). *Dôd*—37 of the 58 occurrences of this word are used in the Song of Songs and translated as "beloved." It is used mostly to describe human love, although God's kindness toward Israel is also described by the word (see Ezekiel 16:8). *Hesed*—often translated "lovingkindness," "steadfast love" "kindness," or unfailing love, is the predominant word used to describe God's love. *Yādîd* carries the meaning of one who is greatly loved, and is primarily employed to describe the nation Israel or individuals as the object of God's special affection. *Raham*—the root word refers to deep love, usually of a "superior" for an "inferior," rooted in some "natural" bond. It con-

notes a feeling of tender mercy or compassion for the helpless or needy. This deep inner feeling is based on some "natural" bond or some strong tie (e.g., mother for child, God for His earthly children). See discussions in R. Laird Harris, Gleason L. Archer, Jr., Bruce K. Waltke, eds., *Theological Wordbook of the Old Testament,* 2 vols. (Chicago: Moody Press, 1980); see articles under *'ahab, 'ohab, 'hābâ* (p. 14), *dôd* (p. 184), *hesed* (pp. 305–307), *yādîd* (p. 364), and *rāham* (pp. 841–843).

2. *Phileo* is found in Revelation 22:15; Matthew 6:5, 10:37; 23:6; Luke 20:46; John 11:3, 36; 1 Corinthans 16:22. Its verbal forms appear in many contexts.

3. Note that the verb *phileo* is never used in a command to men to love God. It is, however, used as a warning in 1 Corinthians 16:22.

4. Compare how it is used for the love of the Father for the Son in John 3:35 (*agape*) and 5:20 (*philos*); the Father's love for the believer in John 14:21 (*agape*) and 16:27 (*philos*); and the Son's love for a certain disciple (the Gospel writer John himself) in John 13:23 (*agape*) and 20:2 (*philos*).

5. Cf. Matthew 10:37; Luke 10:27; Romans 8:28; 1 Corinthians 8:3; 1 Peter 1:8; 1 John.

6. See Romans 13:8-10; James 2:8-12; Matthew 5:17-48.

7. Ecclesiastes 12:13.

8. John 14:15, 21.

12

Picture of Love

"Greater love has no one than this, than to lay down one's life for his friends."
~John 15:13~

Every true religion extols the virtue of love. In this regard, Christianity is no different from all others. In a real sense the Bible is a love book—a book that details how to love God and our fellow human beings, whether friends, neighbors, coworkers, family, or even our enemies.

Jesus Himself summarized the entire Hebrew Scriptures as follows: "'You shall love the Lord your God with all your heart, with all your soul, and with all your mind.' This is the first and great commandment. And the second is like it: 'You shall love your neighbor as yourself.' On these two commandments hang all the Law and the Prophets."[1]

There can be no authentic spirituality without love. Thus, the New Testament lists love as the first in a list of virtues—love, joy, peace, patience, kindness, goodness, faithfulness, gentleness, self-control—and adds that "against such things there is no law."[2] Elsewhere, the apostle Paul writes that of the three enduring virtues—faith, hope, and love—"the greatest of these is love."[3] And the apostle Peter adds that love is the preeminent prerequisite among Christian believers: "*Above all things* have fervent love among yourselves."[4]

This chapter calls attention to some key New Testament passages on love. Together, they give an idea of the nature, source, dimensions, and necessity for love.

The Way of Love

"If I speak in the tongues of men and of angels, but have not love, I am only a resounding gong or a clanging cymbal. If I have the gift of prophecy and can fathom all mysteries and all knowledge, and if I have a faith that can move mountains, but have not love, I am nothing. If I give all I possess to the poor and surrender my body to the flames, but have not love, I gain nothing.

"Love is patient, love is kind. It does not envy, it does not boast, it is not proud. It is not rude, it is not self-seeking, it is not easily angered, it keeps no record of wrongs. Love does not delight in evil but rejoices with the truth. It always protects, always trusts, always hopes, always perseveres.

"Love never fails. But where there are prophecies, they will cease; where there are tongues, they will be stilled; where there is knowledge, it will pass away. For we know in part and we prophesy in part, but when perfection comes, the imperfect disappears. When I was a child, I talked like a child, I thought like a child, I reasoned like a child. When I became a man, I put childish ways behind me. Now we see but a poor reflection as in a mirror; then we shall see face to face. Now I know in part; then I shall know fully, even as I am fully known.

"And now these three remain: faith, hope and love. But the greatest of these is love."—*1 Corinthians 13*

The Source of Love

"But the fruit of the Spirit is love, joy, peace, patience, kindness, goodness, faithfulness, gentleness and self-control. Against such things there is no law."—*Galatians 5:22, 23*

"Dear friends, let us love one another, for love comes from God.

Everyone who loves has been born of God and knows God. Whoever does not love does not know God, because *God is love.* This is how God showed His love among us: He sent His one and only Son into the world that we might live through Him. This is love: not that we loved God, but that He loved us and sent His Son as an atoning sacrifice for our sins.

"Dear friends, since God so loved us, we also ought to love one another. No one has ever seen God; but if we love one another, God lives in us and His love is made complete in us.

"We know that we live in Him and He in us, because He has given us of His Spirit. And we have seen and testify that the Father has sent His Son to be the Savior of the world. If anyone acknowledges that Jesus is the Son of God, God lives in him and he in God. And so we know and rely on the love God has for us.

"*God is love.* Whoever lives in love lives in God, and God in him. In this way, love is made complete among us so that we will have confidence on the Day of Judgment, because in this world we are like Him.

"There is no fear in love. But perfect love drives out fear, because fear has to do with punishment. The one who fears is not made perfect in love.

"We love because He first loved us. If anyone says, 'I love God,' yet hates his brother, he is a liar. For anyone who does not love his brother, whom he has seen, cannot love God, Whom he has not seen. And He has given us this command: Whoever loves God must also love his brother."*—1 John 4:7-21*

The Dimensions of Love

"Who shall separate us from the love of Christ? Shall trouble or hardship or persecution or famine or nakedness or danger or sword? . . . No, in all these things we are more than conquerors through Him Who loved us.

"For I am convinced that neither death nor life, neither angels nor demons, neither the present nor the future, nor any powers, neither height nor depth, nor anything else in all creation, will be able to separate us from the love of God that is in Christ Jesus our Lord."—*Romans 8:35-39*

The Appeal of Love

"Therefore, as God's chosen people, holy and dearly loved, clothe yourselves with compassion, kindness, humility, gentleness and patience. Bear with each other and forgive whatever grievances you may have against one another. Forgive as the Lord forgave you. And over all these virtues put on love, which binds them all together in perfect unity.

"Let the peace of Christ rule in your hearts, since as members of one body you were called to peace. And be thankful. Let the Word of Christ dwell in you richly as you teach and admonish one another with all wisdom, and as you sing psalms, hymns and spiritual songs with gratitude in your hearts to God. And whatever you do, whether in word or deed, do it all in the name of the Lord Jesus, giving thanks to God the Father through Him."—*Colossians 3:12–17*

"I pray that out of His glorious riches He may strengthen you with power through His Spirit in your inner being, so that Christ may dwell in your hearts through faith. And I pray that you, being rooted and established in love, may have power, together with all the saints, to grasp how wide and long and high and deep is the love of Christ, and to know this love that surpasses knowledge—that you may be filled to the measure of all the fullness of God.

"Now to Him Who is able to do immeasurably more than all we ask or imagine, according to His power that is at work within us, to Him be glory in the church and in Christ Jesus throughout all generations, forever and ever! Amen."—*Ephesians 3:16-21.*

Notes:

1. Matthew 22:37-40.
2. Galatians 5:22, 23.
3. 1 Corinthians 13:13.
4. 1 Peter 4:8.

13

Model of Love

"Love is not a matter of counting the years; it's making the years count."
~Wolfman Jack Smith~

Love has furnished the theme for more songs, books, poems, and paintings than any other subject. It has also inspired many heroic deeds and acts of benevolence. Without love, there would not have been so many thousands of schools, hospitals, orphanages, and other great institutions and philanthropic causes.

Love is also that which defines the measure of a person.

Over the centuries, there have been great men and women who have shaped the course of human history. But there is one person whose life and message of love has affected the greatest number of people. That person is the embodiment of love. Thus, as we seek a model of love, it is imperative that we briefly focus on this one incomparable person.

The Embodiment of Love

Over 2,000 years ago one man stepped onto the stage of history and changed it for good. No better words can describe this man than those of James Allen Francis, in his famous 1926 essay titled *One Solitary Life.* This powerful piece, which over the years has seen many different variations, captures the life of Jesus Christ in a few words: Here is my personal adaptation, conflated from many different versions.[1]

He was born in an obscure village, the child of a peasant woman.

He grew up in another obscure village, where

He worked in a carpenter shop until He was thirty.

Then for three years He was an itinerant preacher.

He never owned a home.

He never wrote a book.

He never held an office.

He never had a family.

He never went to college.

He never visited a big city.

He never traveled more than two hundred miles from the place where He was born.

He never did one of the things that accompany greatness.

He had no credentials but Himself.

He was only thirty-three when the tide of public opinion turned against Him.

One of His friends betrayed Him.

Others deserted Him.

One of them denied Him.

He was turned over to His enemies, and

He went through the mockery of a trial.

He was nailed upon a cross between two thieves.

While dying, His executioners gambled for His clothing, the only property he had on earth.

When dead, He was laid in a borrowed grave through the pity of a friend.

But three days later He rose from the dead.
Those are the facts of His human life.
Twenty centuries have come and gone,
And today He is the centerpiece of the human race
And the Leader of mankind's progress.
All the armies that have ever marched,
All the navies that have ever sailed,
All the parliaments that have ever sat, and
All the kings that have ever reigned, put together,
Have not affected the life of mankind on this earth
As powerfully as that One Solitary Life.[2]

Indeed, no other person, army, or movement has affected the people of this earth as much as the *One Solitary Life* of Jesus Christ. And the reason is that His life and mission were the embodiment of God's *agape* love.

Incarnation of Love

The Holy Scriptures define love in terms of God—and God in terms of love. John, the apostle of love, writes: "Whoever does not love does not know God, because *God is love*. . . . No one has ever seen God; but if we love one another, God lives in us and His love is made complete in us. . . . *God is love.* Whoever lives in love lives in God, and God in him" (1 John 4:7, 12, 16, emphasis added).

In other words, love and God are interchangeable. They are essentially indistinguishable. It is as if John is saying, "If you want to know what love is, look at God. And if you want to know what God is like, look at love. For God is love."

The beloved apostle continues by saying that to show us what God is like, God sent His Son Jesus Christ to dwell among us and reveal love to us. This *agape* love—this selfless, sacrificial love—led Jesus Christ to die for us (see 1 John 4:9, 10).

When at one point the disciple Philip said to Jesus, "Lord, show us the Father and that will be enough for us," Jesus answered: "Don't you know Me, Philip, even after I have been among you such a long time? Anyone who has seen Me has seen the Father. How can you say, 'Show us the Father'?"[3]

In short, Jesus was God in human form. Or as theologians put it, He was God incarnate (that is, God in human flesh). Thus, Jesus was a true reflection of love. When we look at Christ (i.e., when we study His character, life, and work), we see love in action. Jesus alone fully demonstrated *agape* love. He was love personified, for He was the perfect Model of love.

A Mission of Love

In describing His earthly mission, Jesus said, "The Spirit of the Lord is on Me, because He has anointed Me to preach Good News to the poor. He has sent Me to proclaim freedom for the prisoners and recovery of sight for the blind, to release the oppressed."[4]

Christ accomplished this mission by healing the sick, helping the needy, and preaching the Good News to them. All of His words and actions were prompted by love.

In the book *Steps to Christ*—a life-changing masterpiece on successful Christian living—the author writes concerning Christ: "Love, mercy, and compassion were revealed in every act of His life. His heart went out in tender sympathy to the children of men. He took man's nature, that He might reach man's wants. The poorest and humblest were not afraid to approach Him. Even little children were attracted to Him. They loved to climb upon His knees and gaze into the pensive face, benignant with love."[5]

The book continues:

"Jesus did not suppress one word of truth,
but He uttered it always in love.

"He exercised the greatest tact and thoughtful, kind
attention in His intercourse with the people.

"He was never rude, never needlessly spoke a

severe word, never gave needless pain to a
sensitive soul.

"He did not censure human weakness.

"He spoke the truth, but always in love.

"He denounced hypocrisy, unbelief, and iniquity; but tears were in His voice as He uttered His scathing rebukes.

"He wept over Jerusalem, the city He loved, which refused
to receive Him, the Way, the Truth, and the Life.
They had rejected Him, the Saviour, but He
regarded them with pitying tenderness.

"His life was one of self-denial and thoughtful
care for others. Every soul was precious in His
eyes. While He ever bore Himself with divine dignity,

"He bowed with the tenderest regard to every member
of the family of God. In all men He saw fallen
souls whom it was His mission to save."[6]

Such is God's character of love as revealed in the life of Christ. It is from the Father's heart that the streams of divine compassion, manifest in Christ, flow out to the children of men. Jesus, the tender, pitying Saviour, was God "manifest in the flesh" (1 Timothy 3:16). If you want to see what love looks like, look at Jesus. He is the Model of true love.

A Pattern of Love

Christ manifested true love in His life of total selflessness. He gave selflessly of His time, His energy, and His life. He was humble, kind, and patient, and never rude. Truly, His love demonstrates the way God loves us. One of the most beautiful pictures painted of Christ is found in the description below:

"Jesus was a perfect Pattern of what we should be.

"He was the strictest observer of His Father's Law,
yet He moved in perfect freedom.

"He had all the fervor of the enthusiast,
yet He was calm, sober, and self-possessed.

"He was elevated above the common affairs of the world,
yet He did not exclude Himself from society.

"He dined with publicans and sinners,

played with little children,

and took them in His arms and blessed them.

"He graced the wedding with His presence.

"He shed tears at the grave of Lazarus.

"He was a lover of the beautiful in nature and
used the lilies to illustrate the value of natural
simplicity in the sight of God, above artificial display.

"He used the occupation of the husbandman to
illustrate the most sublime truths. . . .

"His zeal never degenerated into passion

nor His consistency into selfish obstinacy.

"His benevolence never savored of weakness

nor His sympathy of sentimentalism.

"He combined the innocence and simplicity of the child

with manly strength,

"[He combined an] all-absorbing devotion to God

with tender love for man.

"He possessed commanding dignity

combined with winning grace of humility.

"He manifested unyielding firmness

with gentleness.

"May we live daily in close connection with this perfect, faultless character.

"We have not six patterns to follow, nor five; we have only one, and that is Christ Jesus."[7]

Christ's character of love, depicted in the above statement, reveals what God really is like. For, as the Bible makes abundantly clear, Jesus was God incarnate—God in human form. He was the "only-begotten Son"—a theological phrase that means Jesus was God.[8]

Jesus said: "No one has ever seen God, but God the One and Only [the only-begotten] Who is at the Father's side, has made Him known."[9] On yet another occasion, Christ said: "All things have been committed to Me by My Father. No one knows the Son except the Father, and no one knows the Father except the Son and those to whom the Son chooses to reveal Him."[10]

Display of Love

As a Messenger of love, Christ came to this world as the untiring Servant of man's necessity. He "took our infirmities, and bare our sicknesses" that He might minister to every need of humanity (see Matthew 8:17). Though His work was hard and trying, He did not fail or become discouraged. He was always patient and cheerful—for such is the spirit of love.

Christ displayed love throughout His ministry of healing, teaching, and salvation, helping all who were in sorrow and affliction. In the remainder of this section of our book, I will quote a few sentences from the opening chapter of the book *The Ministry of Healing*, a work that details how Christ models for us how to carry out our work of ministering to people in need.[11]

In His labor of love, Christ reached out to all classes of people with tenderness and courteous grace. "His voice was the first sound that many had ever heard, His name the first word they had ever spoken, His face the first they had ever looked upon."

As a teacher, He spoke profound truths in language so simple that His audience could not fail of understanding. "His instruction was so direct, His illustrations were so appropriate, His words so sympathetic and cheerful, that His hearers were charmed. The simplicity and earnestness with which He addressed the needy, hallowed every word."

But while He ministered to the poor, Jesus also found ways of reaching the rich. Thus, "He sought the acquaintance of the wealthy and cultured Pharisee, the Jewish nobleman, and the Roman ruler. He accepted their invitations, attended their feasts, made Himself familiar with their interests and occupations," in order to "gain access to their hearts, and reveal to them the imperishable riches of God's love."

Jesus also revealed true love in how He related to people in all walks of life. His "work was not restricted to any time," place, or nationality, for "His compassion knew no limit." "He passed by no human being as worthless." He cared for both the poor and the rich, showing no favoritism to class or rank. "He saw the needs of men and women, children and youth, and to all He gave the invitation, 'Come unto Me.'"

Though He was Jewish, Christ "recognized no distinction of nationality or rank or creed." Against the national prejudices of His day, He mingled freely with the despised Samaritans and Gentiles. He accepted their hospitality, slept in their homes, "ate with them at their tables—partaking of the food prepared and served by their hands—taught in their streets, and treated them with the utmost kindness and courtesy. And while He drew their hearts to Him by the tie of human sympathy, His divine grace brought to them the salvation which the Jews rejected."

"The life of Christ established a religion in which there is no caste, a religion by which Jew and Gentile, free and bond, are linked in a common brotherhood, equal before God. No question of policy influenced His movements. He made no difference between neighbors and strangers, friends and enemies. That which appealed to His heart was a soul thirsting for the waters of life."

Truly, Christ was a Model of true love. "He came to show that His gift of mercy and love is as unconfined as the air, the light, or the showers of rain that refresh the earth."[12]

If we look carefully at Christ's life, ministry, and teaching, we cannot help but confess, "This is love!"

Notes:

1. The "One Solitary Life" version reproduced in this chapter is my own, adapted and conflated from many different versions currently in circulation. At the time of writing, a Google search of the Internet using the phrase "One Solitary Life" as a search phrase generated some 38,700

"hits" of different variations of this familiar and well-loved piece. Although many attribute it to an anonymous author, available evidence points to Dr. James Allen Francis as the originator of this work. According to research by the San Joaquin Valley Library System, "One Solitary Life" was first presented by Dr. Francis at the First Baptist Church of Los Angeles in a sermon, "Arise, Sir Knight," delivered on July 11, 1926 to the National Baptist Young Peoples' Union. The piece was later included as the last sermon in his book, *The Real Jesus and Other Sermons* (Philadelphia: Judson Press, 1926), pp. 123, 124. For more on the authorship and versions of the "One Solitary Life" essay, see http://www.sjvls.org/bens/bf007sl.htm.

2. As noted, today many variations of the "One Solitary Life" piece are in circulation (the one in this chapter being my own version). Before the original author, James Allen Francis, died at age 64 on June 30, 1928, he apparently rewrote the "One Solitary Life" story in past tense with several minor changes. Reproduced below is the first printed version, believed to have been given to the National Baptist Young Peoples Union convention on July 11, 1926 (see previous note). Notice that in the original, the phrase, "one solitary life" does not end the piece. Rather, the rest of the paragraph continues with an emphasis upon "great adventures," concluding, "No man has ever done a great thing until he has first believed a great thing." Here's the original version of the "One Solitary Life" essay: "Let us turn now to the story. A child is born in an obscure village. He is brought up in another obscure village. He works in a carpenter shop until he is thirty, and then for three brief years is an itinerant preacher, proclaiming a message and living a life. He never writes a book. He never holds an office. He never raises an army. He never has a family of his own. He never owns a home. He never goes to college. He never travels two hundred miles from the place where he was born. He gathers a little group of friends about him and teaches them his way of life. While still a young man the tide of popular feeling turns against him. The band of followers forsakes him. One denies him; another betrays him. He is turned over to his enemies. He goes through the mockery of a trial; he is nailed on a cross between two thieves, and when dead is laid in a borrowed grave by the kindness of a friend. Those are the facts of his human life. He rises from the dead. Today we look back across nineteen hundred years and ask, What kind of a trail has he left across the centuries? When we try to sum up his influence, all the armies that ever marched, all the parliaments that ever sat, all the kings that ever reigned are absolutely picayune in their influence on mankind compared with that of this *one solitary life*. [Continuing in the same paragraph, Dr. Francis said:] He has changed the moral climate of the world, and he is changing it now, and will continue to do so until the kingdoms of this world shall become the

kingdom of our Lord and of his Christ. I ask you to pause a moment and think of this thing which Christians believe. We are talking about great adventures. I remind you that there must be a great adventure in faith before there can be a great adventure in action. No man has ever done a great thing until he has first believed a great thing" (emphasis mine). For a comparison and discussion of the different versions of "One Solitary Life," see http://www.sjvls.org/bens/bf007sl.htm.

3. John 14:8, 9.
4. Luke 4:18.
5. Ellen G. White, *Steps to Christ,* pp. 11, 12.
6. Ibid., p. 12. Note: I have reformatted the original paragraph so that the pronoun "He" stands out.
7. Ellen G. White, *In Heavenly Places*, p. 54. As in the reference in note 6, I have reformatted the original paragraph so that the pronouns referring to Christ become prominent.
8. In one of his sermons on John 3:16, John Piper beautifully explains the meaning of the phrase, "only-begotten Son." He writes: "In calling the Son of God 'only begotten' Jesus means to distinguish the only begotten Son of God from sons who are made or adopted as sons. The angels are called 'sons of God' (Job 1:6), and we Christians are called 'sons of God' (Rom. 8:14-16). Angels are 'sons of God' by virtue of being directly created by God; and Christians are 'sons of God' by virtue of being adopted into His family through our being joined to Christ by the Holy Spirit. But the 'one and only begotten Son' is not a Son by creation or by adoption, but by begetting. And begetting is simply a human analogy for what is beyond our comprehension. But it carries a crucial truth, as C.S. Lewis said: 'Rabbits beget rabbits; horses beget horses; humans beget humans, not statues or portraits; and God begets God—not humans and not angels. God's only begotten Son is God. And there never was a time when God had not begotten his Son. Because the begetting of the Son is equally eternal with the existence of God the Father. The standing forth of the Son as a perfect, personal image and representation and equal of the Father so that They exist as two Persons with one divine essence is simply what it means to be God. This is the way God has existed from all eternity, without beginning. This is the point of John 1:1, 14, 'In the beginning was the Word, and the Word was with God and the Word was God. . . . And the Word became flesh and dwelt among us.'" See John Piper's sermon "The Design: Love," preached on December 11, 1994; available online at http://www.soundofgrace.com/piper94/12-11-94.htm. For a detailed discussion of the deity of Christ, see J. I. Packer's classic work, *Knowing God* (Downers Grove, Ill.: InterVarsity Press, 1993), pp. 52-64.

9. John 1:18.
10. Matthew 11:27.
11. E. G. White, *The Ministry of Healing*, pp. 17-25.
12. Ibid., p. 25.

PART IV

Love Gems

14

Anatomy of Love

"True love is the parent of humility."
~William Ellery Channing~

Some have said that the greatest, strongest, deepest thing the apostle Paul ever penned was 1 Corinthians 13—the Bible's chapter on love. It is called "The Hymn of Love." Others consider it a lyrical interpretation of the Sermon on the Mount, or "the Beatitudes set to music."

Though thousands of sermons have been written and preached on this chapter, it is generally recognized that the most insightful work on 1 Corinthians 13 is the well-acclaimed classic sermon, *The Greatest Thing in the World,* by the nineteenth-century scientist and evangelist, Henry Drummond. First published in 1880, this classic work has truly stood the test of time.[1]

Unfortunately, many are not aware of the existence of this most valuable gem on love. That is why it is being included in this volume. As you read this timeless sermon, may you be inspired to love as God wants you to love. Love without distinction—without calculation. Love without procrastination. Simply love. Lavish it upon the poor, where it is very easy, and the rich, who often need it most. But most of all, upon our equals, where it is very difficult, and for whom perhaps we each do the least of all.

The Greatest Thing in the World

Everyone has asked himself the great question of antiquity as of the modern world: What is the *summum bonum*—the supreme good? You have life before you. Once only you can live it. What is the noblest object of desire, the supreme gift to covet?

We have been accustomed to be told that the greatest thing in the religious world is Faith. That great word has been the keynote for centuries of the popular religion; and we have easily learned to look upon it as the greatest thing in the world.

Well, we are wrong. If we have been told that, we may miss the mark. In the 13th chapter of I Corinthians, Paul takes us to CHRISTIANITY AT ITS SOURCE and there we see, "The greatest of these is love."

It is not an oversight. Paul was speaking of faith just a moment before. He says, "If I have all faith, so that I can remove mountains, and have not love, I am nothing." So far from forgetting, he deliberately contrasts them, "Now abideth Faith, Hope, Love," and without a moment's hesitation the decision falls, "The greatest of these is Love."

And it is not prejudice. A man is apt to recommend to others his own strong point. Love was not Paul's strong point. The observing student can detect a beautiful tenderness growing and ripening all through his character as Paul gets old; but the hand that wrote, "The greatest of these is love," when we meet it first, is stained with blood.

Nor is this letter to the Corinthians peculiar in singling out love as the *summum bonum*. The masterpieces of Christianity are agreed about it. Peter says, "Above all things have fervent love among yourselves." *Above all things.* And John goes farther, "God is love."

You remember the profound remark which Paul makes elsewhere, "Love is the fulfilling of the Law." Did you ever think what he meant by that? In those days men were working the passage to Heaven by keeping the Ten Commandments, and the hundred and ten other commandments which they had manufactured out of them. Christ came and said, "I will show you a more simple way. If you do one thing, you will do these hundred and ten things, without ever thinking about them. If you *love*, you will unconsciously fulfill the whole Law."

You can readily see for yourselves how that must be so. Take any of the commandments. "Thou shalt have no other gods before Me." If a man love God, you will not require to tell him that. Love is the fulfilling of that law. "Take not His name in vain." Would he ever dream of taking His name in vain if he loved Him? "Remember the Sabbath day to keep it holy." Would he not be too glad to have one day in seven to dedicate more exclusively to the object of his affection? Love would fulfill all these laws regarding God.

And so, if he loved man, you would never think of telling him to honor his father and mother. He could not do anything else. It would be preposterous to tell him not to kill. You could only insult him if you suggested that he should not steal—how could he steal from those he loved? It would be superfluous to beg him not to bear false witness against his neighbor. If he loved him it would be the last thing he would do. And you would never dream of urging him not to covet what his neighbors had. He would rather they possessed it than himself. In this way "Love is the fulfilling of the Law." It is the rule for fulfilling all rules, the new commandment for keeping all the old commandments, Christ's one SECRET OF THE CHRISTIAN LIFE.

Now Paul has learned that; and in this noble eulogy he has given us the most wonderful and original account extant of the *summum bonum*. We may divide it into three parts. In the beginning of the short chapter we have Love *contrasted*; in the heart of it, we have Love *analyzed*; toward the end, we have Love *defended* as the supreme gift.

I. THE CONTRAST

Paul begins by contrasting Love with other things that men in those days thought much of. I shall not attempt to go over these things in detail. Their inferiority is already obvious.

He contrasts it with *eloquence.* And what a noble gift it is, the power of playing upon the souls and wills of men, and rousing them to lofty purposes and holy deeds! Paul says, "If I speak with the tongues of men and of angels, and have not love, I am become sounding brass, or a tinkling cymbal." We all know why. We have all felt the brazenness of words without emotion, the hollowness, the unaccountable unpersuasiveness, of eloquence behind which lies no Love.

He contrasts it with *prophecy.* He contrasts it with *mysteries.* He contrasts it with *faith.* He contrasts it with *charity.* Why is Love greater than faith? Because the end is greater than the means. And why is it greater than charity? Because the whole is greater than the part.

Love is greater than *faith,* because the end is greater than the means. What is the use of having faith? It is to connect the soul with God. And what is the object of connecting man with God? That he may become like God. But God is Love. Hence Faith, the means, is in order to Love, the end. Love, therefore, obviously is greater than faith. "If I have all faith, so as to remove mountains, but have not love, I am nothing."

It is greater than *charity,* again, because the whole is greater than a part. Charity is only a little bit of Love, one of the innumerable avenues of Love, and there may even be, and there is, a great deal of charity without Love. It is a very easy thing to toss a copper to a beggar on the street; it is generally an easier thing than not to do it.

Yet Love is just as often in the withholding. We purchase relief from the sympathetic feelings roused by the spectacle of misery, at the copper's cost. It is too cheap—too cheap for us, and often too dear for the beggar. If we really loved him we would either do more for him, or less. Hence, "If I bestow all my goods to feed the poor, but have not love, it profiteth me nothing."

Then Paul contrasts it with *sacrifice* and martyrdom: "If I give my body to be burned, but have not love, it profiteth me nothing." Missionaries can take nothing greater to the heathen world than the impress and reflection of the Love of God upon their own character. That is the universal language. It will take them years to speak in Chinese, or in the dialects of India. From the day they land, that language of Love, understood by all, will be pouring forth its unconscious eloquence.

It is the man who is the missionary, it is not his words. His character is his message. In the heart of Africa, among the great lakes, I have come across black men and women who remembered the only white man they ever saw before—David Livingstone; and as you cross his footsteps in that dark continent, MEN'S FACES LIGHT UP as they speak of the kind doctor who passed there years ago. They could not understand him; but they felt the love that beat in his heart. They knew that it was love, although he spoke no word.

Take into your sphere of labor, where you also mean to lay down your life, that simple charm, and your lifework must succeed. You can take nothing greater, you need take nothing less. You may take every accomplishment; you may be braced for every sacrifice; but if you give your body to be burned, and have not Love, it will profit you and the cause of Christ *nothing.*

II. THE ANALYSIS

After contrasting Love with these things, Paul, in three verses, very short, gives us an amazing analysis of what this supreme thing is.

I ask you to look at it. It is a compound thing, he tells us. It is like light. As you have seen a man of science take a beam of light and pass it through a crystal prism, as you have seen it come out on the other side of the prism broken up into its component colors—red, and blue, and yellow, and violet, and orange, and all the colors of the rainbow—so Paul passes this thing, Love, through the magnificent prism of his inspired intellect, and it comes out on the other side broken up into its elements.

In these few words we have what one might call THE SPECTRUM OF LOVE, the analysis of Love. Will you observe what its elements are? Will you notice that they have common names; that they are virtues which we hear about every day; that they are things which can be practiced by every man in every place in life; and how, by a multitude of small things and ordinary virtues, the supreme thing, the *summum bonum,* is made up?

The Spectrum of Love has nine ingredients:

Patience	"Love suffereth long"
Kindness	"And is kind"
Generosity	"Love envieth not"
Humility	"Love vaunteth not itself, is not puffed up"
Courtesy	"Doth not behave itself unseemly"
Unselfishness	"Seeketh not its own"
Good temper	"Is not provoked"
Guilelessness	"Taketh not account of evil"
Sincerity	"Rejoiceth not in unrighteousness, but rejoiceth with the truth"

Patience; kindness; generosity; humility; courtesy; unselfishness; good temper; guilelessness; sincerity—these make up the supreme gift, the stature of the perfect man.

You will observe that all are in relation to men, in relation to life, in relation to the known today and the near tomorrow, and not to the unknown eternity. We hear much of love to God; Christ spoke much of love to man. We make a great deal of peace with Heaven; Christ made much of peace on Earth. Religion is not a strange or added thing, but the inspiration of the secular life, the breathing of an Eternal Spirit through this temporal world. The supreme thing, in short, is not a thing at all, but the giving of a further finish to the multitudinous words and acts which make up the sum of every common day.

Patience. This is the normal attitude of love; Love passive, Love waiting to begin; not in a hurry; calm; ready to do its work when the summons comes, but meantime wearing the ornament of a meek and quiet spirit. Love suffers long; beareth all things; believeth all things; hopeth all things. For Love understands, and therefore waits.

Kindness. Love active. Have you ever noticed how much of Christ's life was spent in doing kind things—in *merely* doing kind things? Run over it with that in view, and you will find that He spent a great proportion of His time simply in making people happy, in DOING GOOD TURNS to people. There is only one thing greater than happiness in the world, and that is holiness; and it is not in our keeping; but what God *has* put in our power is the happiness of those about us, and that is largely to be secured by our being kind to them.

"The greatest thing," says someone, "a man can do for his Heavenly Father is to be kind to some of His other children." I wonder why it is that we are not all kinder than we are? How much the world needs it! How easily it is done! How instantaneously it acts! How infallibly it is remembered! How superabundantly it pays itself back—for there is no debtor in the world so honorable, so superbly honorable, as Love. "Love never faileth." Love is success, Love is happiness, Love is life. "Love," I say with Browning, "is energy of life."

"For life, with all it yields of joy or woe
And hope and fear,
Is just our chance o' the prize of learning love,—
How love might be, hath been indeed, and is."

Where Love is, God is. He that dwelleth in Love dwelleth in God. God is Love. Therefore *love.* Without distinction, without calculation, without procrastination, love. Lavish it upon the poor, where it is very easy; especially upon the rich, who often need it most; most of all upon our equals, where it is very difficult, and for whom perhaps we each do least of all.

There is a difference between *trying to please* and *giving pleasure.* Give pleasure. Lose no chance of giving pleasure; for that is the ceaseless and anonymous triumph of a truly loving spirit. "I shall pass through this world but once. Any good thing, therefore, that I can do, or any kindness that I can show to any human being, let me do it now. Let me not defer it or neglect it, for I shall not pass this way again."

Generosity. "Love envieth not." This is Love in competition with others. Whenever you attempt a good work you will find other men doing the same kind of work, and probably doing it better. Envy them not. Envy is a feeling of ill will to those who are in the same line as ourselves, a spirit of covetousness and detraction. How little Christian work even is a protection against un-Christian feeling! That most despicable of all the unworthy moods which cloud a Christian's soul assuredly waits for us on the threshold of every work, unless we are fortified with this grace of magnanimity. Only one thing truly need the Christian envy—the large, rich, generous soul which "envieth not."

And then, after having learned all that, you have to learn this further thing, *Humility*—to put a seal upon your lips and forget what you have done. After you have been kind, after Love has stolen forth into the world and done its beautiful work, go back into the shade again and say nothing about it. Love hides even from itself. Love waives even self-satisfaction. "Love vaunteth not itself, is not puffed up." Humility—Love hiding.

[Courtesy.] The fifth ingredient is a somewhat strange one to find in this *summum bonum*: *Courtesy*. This is Love in society, Love in relation to etiquette. "Love does not behave itself unseemly."

Politeness has been defined as love in trifles. Courtesy is said to be love in little things. And the one secret of politeness is to love.

Love *cannot* behave itself unseemly. You can put the most untutored persons into the highest society, and if they have a reservoir of Love in their heart they will not behave themselves unseemly. They simply cannot do it. Carlisle said of Robert Burns that there was no truer gentleman in Europe than the ploughman-poet. It was because he loved everything—the mouse, and the daisy, and all the things, great and small, that God had made. So with this simple passport he could mingle with any society, and enter courts and palaces from his little cottage on the banks of the Ayr.

You know the meaning of the word "gentleman." It means a gentle man—a man who does things gently, with Love. That is the whole art and mystery of it. The gentle man cannot in the nature of things do an ungentle, an ungentlemanly thing. The ungentle soul, the inconsiderate, unsympathetic nature, cannot do anything else. "Love doth not behave itself unseemly."

Unselfishness. "Love seeketh not her own." Observe: Seeketh not even that which is her own. In Britain the Englishman is devoted, and rightly, to his rights. But there come times when a man may exercise even THE HIGHER RIGHT of giving up his rights.

Yet Paul does not summon us to give up our rights. Love strikes much deeper. It would have us not seek them at all, ignore them, eliminate the personal element altogether from our calculations.

It is not hard to give up our rights. They are often eternal. The difficult thing is to give up *ourselves*. The more difficult thing still is not to seek things for ourselves at all. After we have sought them, bought them, won them, deserved them, we have taken the cream off them for ourselves already. Little cross then to give them up. But not to seek them, to look every man not on his own things, but on the things of others—that is the difficulty. "Seekest thou great things for thyself?" said the prophet; *"seek them not."* Why? Because there is no greatness in *things*. Things cannot be great. The only greatness is unselfish love. Even self-denial in itself is nothing, is almost a mistake. Only a great purpose or a mightier love can justify the waste.

It is more difficult, I have said, not to seek our own at all than, having sought it, to give it up. I must take that back. It is only true of a partly selfish heart. Nothing is a hardship to Love, and nothing is hard. I believe that Christ's "yoke" is easy. Christ's yoke is just His way of taking life. And I believe it is an easier way than any other. I believe it is a happier way than any other. The most obvious lesson in Christ's teaching is that there is no happiness in having and getting anything, but only in giving.

I repeat, *there is no happiness in having or in getting, but only in giving.* Half the world is on the wrong scent in pursuit of happiness.

They think it consists in having and getting, and in being served by others. It consists in giving, and in serving others. "He that would be great among you," said Christ, "let him serve." He that would be happy, let him remember that there is but one way—"it is more blessed, it is more happy, to give than to receive."

[Good Temper.] The next ingredient is a very remarkable one: *Good temper.* "Love is not provoked."

Nothing could be more striking than to find this here. We are inclined to look upon bad temper as a very harmless weakness. We speak of it as a mere infirmity of nature, a family failing, a matter of temperament, not a thing to take into very serious account in estimating a man's character. And yet here, right in the heart of this analysis of Love, it finds a place; and the Bible again and again returns to condemn it as one of the most destructive elements in human nature.

The peculiarity of ill temper is that it is the vice of the virtuous. It is often the one blot on an otherwise noble character. You know men who are all but perfect, and women who would be entirely perfect, but for an easily ruffled, quick-tempered, or "touchy" disposition. This compatibility of ill temper with high moral character is one of the strangest and saddest problems of ethics.

The truth is, there are two great classes of sins—sins of the *Body* and sins of the *Disposition*. The Prodigal Son may be taken as a type of the first, the Elder Brother of the second. Now, society has no doubt whatever as to which of these is the worse. Its brand falls, without a challenge, upon the Prodigal. But are we right? We have no balance to weigh one another's sins, and coarser and finer are but human words; but faults in the higher nature may be less venal than those in the lower, and to the eye of Him Who is Love, a sin against Love may seem a hundred times more base.

No form of vice, not worldliness, not greed of gold, not drunkenness itself, does more to un-Christianize society than evil temper. For embittering life, for breaking up communities, for destroying the most sacred relationships, for devastating homes, for withering up men and women, for taking the bloom of childhood, in short,

FOR SHEER GRATUITOUS MISERY-PRODUCING POWER this influence stands alone.

Look at the Elder Brother—moral, hard-working, patient, dutiful—let him get all credit for his virtues—look at this man, this baby, sulking outside his own father's door. "He was angry," we read, "and would not go in." Look at the effect upon the father, upon the servants, upon the happiness of the guests. Judge of the effect upon the Prodigal—and how many prodigals are kept out of the Kingdom of God by the unlovely character of those who profess to be inside. Analyze, as a study in Temper, the thundercloud itself as it gathers upon the Elder Brother's brow. What is it made of? Jealousy, anger, pride, uncharity, cruelty, self-righteousness, touchiness, doggedness, sullenness—these are the ingredients of this dark and loveless soul. In varying proportions, also, these are the ingredients of all ill temper. Judge if such sins of the disposition are not worse to live in, and for others to live with, than the sins of the body.

Did Christ indeed not answer the question Himself when He said, "I say unto you that the publicans and the harlots go into the Kingdom of Heaven before you"? There is really no place in Heaven for a disposition like this. A man with such a mood could only make Heaven miserable for all the people in it. Except, therefore, such a man be BORN AGAIN, he cannot, simply *cannot*, enter the Kingdom of Heaven.

You will see then why Temper is significant. It is not in what it is alone, but in what it reveals. This is why I speak of it with such unusual plainness. It is a test for love, a symptom, a revelation of an unloving nature at bottom. It is the intermittent fever which bespeaks unintermittent disease within; the occasional bubble escaping to the surface which betrays some rottenness underneath; a sample of the most hidden products of the soul dropped involuntarily when off one's guard; in a word, the lightning form of a hundred hideous and un-Christian sins. A want of patience, a want of kindness, a want of generosity, a want of courtesy, a want of unselfishness, are all instantaneously symbolized in one flash of Temper.

Hence it is not enough to deal with the Temper. We must go to the source, and change the inmost nature, and the angry humors [characteristics] will die away of themselves. Souls are made sweet not by taking the acid fluids out, but by putting something in—a great Love, a new Spirit, the Spirit of Christ. Christ, the Spirit of Christ, interpenetrating ours, sweetens, purifies, transforms all. This only can eradicate what is wrong, work a chemical change, renovate and regenerate, and rehabilitate the inner man. Willpower does not change men. Time does not change men. CHRIST DOES. Therefore, "Let that mind be in you which was also in Christ Jesus."

Some of us have not much time to lose. Remember, once more, that this is a matter of life or death. I cannot help speaking urgently, for myself, for yourselves. "Whoso shall offend one of these little ones, which believe in Me, it were better for him that a millstone were hanged about his neck, and that he were drowned in the depth of the sea." That is to say, it is the deliberate verdict of the Lord Jesus that it is better not to live than not to love. *It is better not to live than not to love.*

[Guilelessness and Sincerity.] *Guilelessness* and *Sincerity* may be dismissed almost without a word. Guilelessness is the grace for suspicious people. The possession of it is THE GREAT SECRET OF PERSONAL INFLUENCE.

You will find, if you think for a moment, that the people who influence you are people who believe in you. In an atmosphere of suspicion men shrivel up; but in that atmosphere they expand, and find encouragement and educative fellowship.

It is a wonderful thing that here and there in this hard, uncharitable world there should still be left a few rare souls who think no evil. This is the great unworldliness. Love "thinketh no evil," imputes no motive, sees the bright side, puts the best construction on every action. What a delightful state of mind to live in! What a stimulus and benediction even to meet with it for a day! To be trusted is to be saved. And if we try to influence or elevate others, we shall soon see that success is in proportion to their belief of our belief in them. The respect of another is the first restoration of the self-respect a man has lost; our ideal of what he is becomes to him the hope and pattern of what he may become.

"Love rejoiceth not in unrighteousness, but rejoiceth with the truth." I have called this *Sincerity* from the words rendered in the

Authorized Version by "rejoiceth in the truth." And, certainly, were this the real translation, nothing could be more just; for he who loves will love Truth not less than men. He will rejoice in the Truth—rejoice not in what he has been taught to believe; not in this church's doctrine or in that; not in this ism or in that ism; but "in *the Truth*." He will accept only what is real; he will strive to get at facts; he will search for *Truth* with a humble and unbiased mind, and cherish whatever he finds at any sacrifice.

But the more literal translation of the Revised Version calls for just such a sacrifice for truth's sake here. For what Paul really meant is, as we there read, "Rejoiceth not in unrighteousness, but rejoiceth with the truth," a quality which probably no one English word—and certainly not *Sincerity*—adequately defines. It includes, perhaps more strictly, the self-restraint which refuses to make capital out of others' faults; the charity which delights not in exposing the weakness of others, but "covereth all things"; the sincerity of purpose which endeavors to see things as they are, and rejoices to find them better than suspicion feared or calumny denounced.

[Learning to Love]

So much for the analysis of Love. Now the business of our lives is to have these things fitted into our characters. That is the supreme work to which we need to address ourselves in this world, to learn Love. Is life not full of opportunities for learning Love? Every man and woman every day has a thousand of them. The world is not a playground; it is a schoolroom. Life is not a holiday, but an education. And THE ONE ETERNAL LESSON for us all is *how better we can love.*

What makes a man a good cricketer? Practice. What makes a man a good artist, a good sculptor, a good musician? Practice. What makes a man a good linguist, a good stenographer? Practice. What makes a man a good man? Practice. Nothing else. There is nothing capricious about religion. We do not get the soul in different ways, under different laws, from those in which we get the body and the mind.

If a man does not exercise his arm he develops no biceps muscle;

and if a man does not exercise his soul, he acquires no muscle in his soul, no strength of character, no vigor of moral fibre, no beauty of spiritual growth. Love is not a thing of enthusiastic emotion. It is a rich, strong, manly, vigorous expression of the whole round Christian character—the Christlike nature in its fullest development. And the constituents of this great character are only to be built up by CEASELESS PRACTICE.

What was Christ doing in the carpenter's shop? Practicing. Though perfect, we read that He *learned* obedience, and grew in wisdom and in favor with God. Do not quarrel, therefore, with your lot in life. Do not complain of its never-ceasing cares, its petty environment, the vexations you have to stand, the small and sordid souls you have to live and work with.

Above all, do not resent temptation; do not be perplexed because it seems to thicken round you more and more, and ceases neither for effort nor for agony nor prayer. That is your practice. That is the practice which God appoints you; and it is having its work in making you patient, and humble, and generous, and unselfish, and kind, and courteous. Do not grudge the hand that is moulding the still too shapeless image within you. It is growing more beautiful, though you see it not; and every touch of temptation may add to its perfection.

Therefore keep in the midst of life. Do not isolate yourself. Be among men and among things, and among troubles, and difficulties, and obstacles. You remember Goethe's words: "Talent develops itself in solitude; character in the stream of life." Talent develops itself in solitude—the talent of prayer, of faith, of meditation, of seeing the unseen; character grows in the stream of the world's life. That chiefly is where men are to learn Love.

How? Now, how? To make it easier, I have named a few of the elements of Love. But these are only elements. Love itself can never be defined. Light is a something more than the sum of its ingredients—a glowing, dazzling, tremulous ether. And Love is something more than all its elements—a palpitating, quivering, sensitive, living thing. By synthesis of all the colors, men can make whiteness, they cannot make light. By synthesis of all the virtues, men can make virtue, they cannot make Love.

How then are we to have this transcendent living whole conveyed into our souls? We brace our wills to secure it. We try to copy those who have it. We lay down rules about it. We watch. We pray. But these things alone will not bring Love into our nature. Love is an *effect*. And only as we fulfill the right condition can we have the effect produced. Shall I tell you what the *cause* is?

If you turn to the Revised Version of the First Epistle of John you find these words: "We love because He first loved us." "We love," not "We love *Him*." That is the way the old version has it, and it is quite wrong. "*We love*—because He first loved us." Look at that word "because." It is the *cause* of which I have spoken. "*Because* He first loved us," the effect follows that we love, we love Him, we love all men. We cannot help it. Because He loved us, we love, we love everybody. Our heart is slowly changed.

Contemplate the Love of Christ, and you will love. Stand before that mirror, reflect Christ's character, and you will be changed into the same image from tenderness to tenderness. There is no other way. You cannot love to order. You can only look at the lovely object, and fall in love with it, and grow into likeness to it. And so look at this Perfect Character, this Perfect Life. Look at THE GREAT SACRIFICE as He laid down Himself, all through life, and upon the Cross of Calvary; and you must love Him. And loving Him, you must become like Him.

Love begets Love. It is a process of induction. Put a piece of iron in the presence of an electrified body, and that piece of iron for a time becomes electrified. It is changed into a temporary magnet in the mere presence of a permanent magnet, and as long as you leave the two side by side, they are both magnets alike. Remain side by side with Him Who loved us, and GAVE HIMSELF FOR US, and you, too, will become a permanent magnet, a permanently attractive force; and like Him you will draw all men unto you, like Him you will be drawn unto all men. That is the inevitable effect of Love. Any man who fulfills that cause must have that effect produced in him.

Try to give up the idea that religion comes to us by chance, or by mystery, or by caprice. It comes to us by natural law, or by supernatural law, for all law is Divine.

Edward Irving went to see a dying boy once, and when he entered the room he just put his hand on the sufferer's head, and said, "My boy, God loves you," and went away. The boy started from his bed, and called out to the people in the house,

"God loves me! God loves me!"

One word! It changed that boy. The sense that God loved him overpowered him, melted him down, and began the creating of a new heart in him. And that is how the Love of God melts down the unlovely heart in man, and begets in him the new creature, who is patient and humble and gentle and unselfish. And there is no other way to get it. There is no mystery about it. We love others, we love everybody, we love our enemies, *because He first loved us.*

III. THE DEFENCE

Now I have a closing sentence or two to add about Paul's reason for singling out Love as the supreme possession.

It is a very remarkable reason. In a single word it is this: *it lasts.* "Love," urges Paul, "never faileth." Then he begins again one of his marvelous lists of the great things of the day, and exposes them one by one. He runs over the things that men thought were going to last, and shows that they are all fleeting, temporary, passing away.

"Whether there be *prophecies,* they shall be done away." It was the mother's ambition for her boy in those days that he should become a prophet. For hundreds of years God had never spoken by means of any prophet, and at that time the prophet was greater than the king. Men waited wistfully for another messenger to come, and hung upon his lips when he appeared, as upon the very voice of God. Paul says, "Whether there be prophecies, they shall fail." The Bible is full of prophecies. One by one they have "failed"; that is, having been fulfilled, their work is finished; they have nothing more to do now in the world except to feed a devout man's faith.

Then Paul talks about *tongues.* That was another thing that was greatly coveted. "Whether there be tongues, they shall cease." As we all know, many, many centuries have passed since tongues have been known in this world. They have ceased. Take it in any sense you like. Take it, for illustration merely, as languages in general—a sense which was not in Paul's mind at all, and which though it cannot give us the specific lesson, will point the general truth.[2]

Consider the words in which these chapters were written—Greek. It has gone. Take the Latin—the other great tongue of those days. It ceased long ago. Look at the Indian language. It is ceasing. The language of Wales, of Ireland, of the Scottish Highlands is dying before our eyes. The most popular book in the English tongue at the present time, except the Bible, is one of Dickens's works, his *Pickwick Papers*. It is largely written in the language of London street life; and experts assure us that in fifty years it will be unintelligible to the average English reader.

Then Paul goes farther, and with even greater boldness adds, "Whether there be *knowledge*, it shall be done away." The wisdom of the ancients, where is it? It is wholly gone. A schoolboy today knows more than Sir Isaac Newton knew; his knowledge has vanished away. You put yesterday's newspaper in the fire: its knowledge has vanished away. You buy the old editions of the great encyclopædias for a few cents: their knowledge has vanished away. Look how the coach has been superseded by the use of steam. Look how electricity has superseded that, and swept a hundred almost new inventions into oblivion. One of the greatest living authorities, Sir William Thompson, said in Scotland, at a meeting at which I was present, "The steam engine is passing away."

"Whether there be knowledge, it shall vanish away." At every workshop you will see, in the backyard, a heap of old iron, a few wheels, a few levers, a few cranks, broken and eaten with rust. Twenty years ago that was the pride of the city. Men flocked in from the country to see the great invention; now it is superseded, its day is done. And all the boasted science and philosophy of this day will soon be old.

In my time, in the University of Edinburgh, the greatest figure in the faculty was Sir James Simpson, the discoverer of chloroform. Recently his successor and nephew, Professor Simpson, was asked by the librarian of the University to go to the library and pick out the books on his subject (midwifery) that were no longer needed. His reply to the librarian was this:

"Take every textbook that is more than ten years old and put it down in the cellar."

Sir James Simpson was a great authority only a few years ago: men came from all parts of the earth to consult him; and almost the whole teaching of that time is consigned by the science of today to oblivion. And in every branch of science it is the same. "Now we know in part. We see through a glass darkly." Knowledge does not last.

Can you tell me anything that is going to last? Many things Paul did not condescend to name. He did not mention money, fortune, fame; but he picked out the great things of his time, the things the best men thought had something in them, and brushed them peremptorily aside. Paul had no charge against these things in themselves. All he said about them was that they would not last. They were great things, but not supreme things. There were things beyond them.

What we are stretches past what we do, beyond what we possess. Many things that men denounce as sins are not sins; but they are temporary. And that is a favorite argument of the New Testament. John says of the world, not that it is wrong, but simply that it "passeth away." There is a great deal in the world that is delightful and beautiful; there is a great deal in it that is great and engrossing; but IT WILL NOT LAST.

All that is in the world, the lust of the eye, the lust of the flesh, and the pride of life, are but for a little while. Love not the world therefore. Nothing that it contains is worth the life and consecration of an immortal soul.[3'] The immortal soul must give itself to something that is immortal. And the only immortal things are these: "Now abideth faith, hope, love, but the greatest of these is love."

Some think the time may come when two of these three things will also pass away—faith into sight, hope into fruition. Paul does not say so. We know but little now about the conditions of the life that is to come. But what is certain is that Love must last. God, the Eternal God, is Love. Covet, therefore, that everlasting gift, that one thing which it is certain is going to stand, that one coinage which will be current in the Universe when all the other coinages of all the nations of the world shall be useless and unhonored.

You will give yourselves to many things, give yourself first to Love. Hold things in their proportion. *Hold things in their proportion.* Let at least the first great object of our lives be to achieve the character defended in these words, the character—and it is the character of Christ—which is built round Love.

I have said this thing is eternal. Did you ever notice how continually John associates Love and faith with eternal life? I was not told when I was a boy that "God so loved the world, that He gave His Only-Begotten Son, that whosoever believeth in Him should have everlasting life." What I was told, I remember, was, that God so loved the world that, if I trusted in Him, I was to have a thing called peace, or I was to have rest, or I was to have joy, or I was to have safety. But I had to find out for myself that whosoever trusteth in Him—that is, whosoever loveth Him, for trust is only the avenue to Love—hath EVERLASTING LIFE.

The Gospel offers a man a life. Never offer a man a thimbleful of Gospel. Do not offer them merely joy, or merely peace, or merely rest, or merely safety; tell them how Christ came to give men a more abundant life than they have, a life abundant in Love, and therefore abundant in salvation for themselves, and large in enterprise for the alleviation and redemption of the world. Then only can the Gospel take hold of the whole of a man, body, soul and spirit, and give to each part of his nature its exercise and reward.

Many of the current Gospels are addressed only to a part of man's nature. They offer peace, not life; faith, not Love; justification, not regeneration. And men slip back again from such religion because it has never really held them. Their nature was not all in it. It offered no deeper and gladder life current than the life that was lived before. Surely it stands to reason that only a fuller Love can compete with the love of the world.

To love abundantly is to live abundantly, and to love forever is to live forever. Hence, eternal life is inextricably bound up with Love. We want to live forever for the same reason that we want to live tomorrow. Why do we want to live tomorrow? Is it because there is someone who loves you, and whom you want to see tomorrow, and be with, and love back? There is no other reason why we should live on than that we love and are beloved. It is when a man has no one to love him that he commits suicide. So long as he has friends, those who love him and whom he loves, he will live, because to live is to love. Be it but the love of a dog, it will keep him in life; but let that go, he has no contact with life, no reason to live. He dies by his own hand.

Eternal life also is to know God, and God is love. This is Christ's Own definition. Ponder it. "This is life eternal, that they might know Thee the only true God, and Jesus Christ Whom Thou hast sent." Love must be eternal. It is what God is. On the last analysis, then, Love is life. Love never faileth, and life never faileth, so long as there is Love.

That is the philosophy of what Paul is showing us; the reason why in the nature of things Love should be the supreme thing—because it is going to last; because in the nature of things it is an Eternal Life. It is a thing that we are living now, not that we get when we die; that we shall have a poor chance of getting when we die unless we are living now. NO WORSE FATE can befall a man in this world than to live and grow old alone, unloving and unloved. To be lost is to live in an unregenerate condition, loveless and unloved; and to be saved is to love; and he that dwelleth in love dwelleth already in God. For God is Love.

[Final Thoughts]

Now I have all but finished. How many of you will join me in reading this chapter once a week for the next three months? A man did that once and it changed his whole life. Will you do it? It is for the greatest thing in the world. You might begin by reading it every day, especially the verses which describe the perfect character. "Love suffereth long, and is kind; love envieth not; love vaunteth not itself."

Get these ingredients into your life. Then everything that you do is eternal. It is worth doing. It is worth giving time to. No man can become a saint in his sleep; and to fulfill the condition required demands a certain amount of prayer and meditation and time, just as improvement in any direction, bodily or mental, requires preparation and care. Address yourselves to that one thing; at any cost have this transcendent character exchanged for yours.

You will find as you look back upon your life that the moments that stand out, the moments when you have really lived, are the moments when you have done things in a spirit of Love. As memory scans the past, above and beyond all the transitory pleasures of life, there leap forward those supreme hours when you have been enabled to do unnoticed kindnesses to those round about you, things too trifling to speak about, but which you feel have entered into your eternal life.

I have seen almost all the beautiful things God has made; I have enjoyed almost every pleasure that He has planned for man; and yet as I look back I see standing out above all the life that has gone four or five short experiences, when the love of God reflected itself in some poor imitation, some small act of love of mine, and these seem to be the things which alone of all one's life abide. Everything else in all our lives is transitory. Every other good is visionary. But the acts of love which no man knows about, or can ever know about—they never fail.

In the Book of Matthew, where the Judgment Day is depicted for us in the imagery of One seated upon a throne and dividing the sheep from the goats, the test of a man then is not, "How have I believed?" but "How have I loved?" The test of religion, the final test of religion, is not religiousness, but Love. I say the final test of religion at that great Day is not religiousness, but Love; not what I have done, not what I have believed, not what I have achieved, but how I have discharged the common charities of life.

Sins of commission in that awful indictment are not even referred to. By what we have not done, *by sins of omission*, we are judged. It could not be otherwise. For the withholding of love is the negation of the Spirit of Christ, the proof that we never knew Him, that for us He lived in vain. It means that He suggested nothing in all our thoughts, that He inspired nothing in all our lives, that we were not once near enough to Him, to be seized with the spell of His compassion for the world. It means that—

"I lived for myself, I thought for myself,
For myself, and none beside—
Just as if Jesus had never lived,
As if He had never died."

Thank God the Christianity of today is coming nearer the world's need. Live to help that on. Thank God men know better, by a hair's breadth, what religion is, what God is, Who Christ is, where Christ is. Who is Christ? He Who fed the hungry, clothed the naked, visited the sick. And where is Christ? Where?—"Whoso shall receive a little child in My name receiveth Me." And who are Christ's? "Everyone that loveth is born of God."

Notes:

1. Henry Drummond (1851–1897), a Scottish evangelist and lecturer, was born in Sterling, Scotland, on August 7, 1851. He was educated at Edinburgh University and in 1877 became a lecturer on science at the Free Church College of Glasgow. He was a geologist and explorer, spending a portion of his time away from the classroom on scientific expeditions. As a Christian, he combined his knowledge of science with his understanding of the Creator and His many creations. He was closely associated with Dwight L. Moody in many of his revival missions in England and Ireland. It was through this association that Moody greatly encouraged Drummond to share his heartfelt thoughts on biblical love. Moody was so impressed by the address that, after its publication, he had it read to his students each year. Although Drummond published several books for the science world, none has reached the fame or endured as has *The Greatest Thing in the World* (London: Hodder & Stoughton Ltd., updated edition, 1920). The book was first published in 1880. Notice that for ease of reading, I have added two subheadings to the original text ("Learning to Love" and "Final Thoughts"), and in two dozen or so places I have divided longer paragraphs into shorter ones. But the text itself has been preserved as the author first published it in 1880.
2. The gift of tongues is one of the many spiritual gifts that the Holy Spirit imparts to believers. However, Christian opinion is divided over key issues relative to the question of tongues. Among these are: (1) whether or not the biblical gift of tongues passed away with the death of the apostles, (2) the purpose for the gift of tongues, (3) whether all believers are to speak in tongues, (4) the qualification necessary to receive the gift of tongues, and (5) the exact nature of biblical tongues. The following scriptural passages will shed some light on whether or not this particular spiritual gift has ceased today: Mark 16:15-18; cf. Matthew 28:18-20; Revelation 14:6; 1 Corinthians 12. The Bible explains the purpose for the gift of tongues in

these passages: Acts 1:8; Ephesians 4:11-14; 1 Corinthians 12:7. As to whether every believer must speak in tongues, these texts provide a definitive answer: 1 Corinthians 12:4-11, 14-19, 28-30; cf. Rom 12:3-8). The Bible also provides some answers on who qualifies to receive any of the spiritual gifts, including the gift of tongues: Acts 2:38; Luke 11:9-13; Acts 5:32; John 14:15, 16. There is considerable debate among Christians over the exact nature of tongues. At issue is this: Is the biblical gift of tongues an ecstatic gibberish (a language incomprehensible both to the speaker and the hearer)—or is it rather a foreign language supernaturally given by God to enable believers to communicate the gospel and build up the church? The disagreement seems to arise from two apparently conflicting passages in 1 Corinthians 14. Those who favor the former view tend to base it on 1 Corithians 14:2, 14, and those who believe in the latter position call attention to 1 Corinthians 14:6-18. Notice, however, that if we adopt the principle of allowing the Bible to interpret itself, and if we try to interpret obscure (or apparently confusing) biblical passages by clear biblical passages on the same subject, the apparent conflict in 1 Corinthians 14 will not be as problematic as we think. By carefully studying the nature of the "tongues" in every occurrence, we can ascertain whether or not speaking in tongues is unintelligible or intelligible. The following are all the known occurrences of tongues outside of the 1 Corinthians 14 passage: Acts 2:1-11; 10:44-47; 11:15-17; and (in Caesarea) 19:1-7. It is worthy of note that the Greek word *glossa,* translated "tongues" in 1 Cor. 14, is the same word employed with reference to the events in the book of Acts. Also, Paul was present in Ephesus when during his ministry twelve followers of John the Baptist spoke in tongues (Acts 19). It was from the same city of Ephesus that he wrote his letter to the Corinthians.

3. According to the Bible, human beings do not have immortality, for "only God has immortality" (1 Timothy 6:16). Presently, we "seek immortality" (Romans 2:7). We shall receive this gift when Jesus comes again: "Behold, I show you a mystery; we shall not all sleep, but we shall all be changed, in a moment, in the twinkling of an eye, at the last trump: for the trumpet shall sound, and the dead shall be raised incorruptible, and we shall be changed. For this corruptible must put on incorruption, and this mortal must put on immortality. So when this corruptible shall have put on incorruption, and this mortal shall have put on immortality, then shall be brought to pass the saying that is written, Death is swallowed up in victory" (1 Corinthians 15:51-54). The Bible uses the word *soul* 1,600 times but never once uses "immortal soul." A human being doesn't *have* a soul but simply *is* a soul: "And the Lord God formed man of the dust of the ground,

and breathed into his nostrils the breath of life; and man became a living soul" (Genesis 2:7). Man became a living soul, i.e., we don't *have* souls but *are* souls. And the Bible teaches that souls (i.e., human beings) are not immortal, but do die or can be destroyed: "The soul that sins shall die" (Ezekiel 18:4, 20; cf. Matthew 10:28; Acts 3:23).

15

PROOF OF LOVE

"True love is spelled G-I-V-E. It is not based on what you can get, but rooted in what you can give to the other person."
~Josh McDowell~

We have noted earlier, in chapter 11, that true love—*agape* love—is a selfless, sacrificial love. It is a love that gives—willingly and generously giving of its time, possessions, abilities, and comforts. True love is willing to sacrifice anything—everything, including life itself—for the sake of the beloved.

Since we have also noted that God is love, the question before us is—what is the proof of His love?

WHAT IS THE PROOF?

The Bible answers: *"For God so loved the world, that He gave His only-begotten Son,* that whosoever believeth in Him should not perish, but have everlasting life" (John 3:16, emphasis added).

The little word *so* in John 3:16 doesn't simply mean an amount of love, but rather a way of loving. In other words, the text doesn't just mean God loved so *much,* but also that God loved *this way.* "God so loved" means "God thus loved."

If we ask, "How? What is the way God loved?" the answer is: He loved in such a way "that He gave His Only-Begotten Son." This giving was a giving up to rejection and death. "He came to His own, and His own received Him not" (John 1:11). Instead, they killed Him.

So when the Father gave His Only-Begotten Son, He gave Him to die. God loved so much that we, who were the very object of His love, turned around and inflicted a fatal wound upon His Son. Love was costly.

But do we fully understand the cost of divine love?

The account that follows is, perhaps, the most vivid account of the proof of love, for it reveals the ultimate giving of God—the giving of Himself on Calvary. Like the work in the previous chapter, this gem on love was also written by another nineteenth-century devotional Christian author, Ellen G. White (1827–1915), whose writings spanned the work of religious contemporaries such as Charles Spurgeon and Oswald Chambers.[1] Based on Matthew 27:31-53, Mark 15:20-38, Luke 23:26-46, and John 19:16-30, this account is taken from the book *The Desire of Ages* (first published in 1898)—a work judged by millions as the best devotional work on the life of Christ.[2] It is supplemented by another selection from her book *Steps to Christ* (first published in 1892)—a life-changing masterpiece on successful Christian living.

As you reflect on the events of Calvary, you will learn how God gave—gave His most, His best, and His all. Calvary is the proof and heart of God's infinite love. Let's now journey back in time to a hill called Calvary.

CALVARY[3]

"And when they were come to the place, which is called Calvary, there they crucified Him."

"That He might sanctify the people with His Own blood," Christ "suffered without the gate." Hebrews 13:12. For transgression of the Law of God, Adam and Eve were banished from Eden. Christ, our Substitute, was to suffer without the boundaries of Jerusalem. He died outside the gate, where felons and murderers were executed. Full of significance are the words, "Christ hath redeemed us from the curse of the Law, being made a curse for us." Galatians 3:13.

A vast multitude followed Jesus from the judgment hall to Calvary. The news of His condemnation had spread throughout Jerusalem, and people of all classes and all ranks flocked toward the place of crucifixion. The priests and rulers had been bound by a promise not to molest Christ's followers if He Himself were delivered to them, and the disciples and believers from the city and the surrounding region joined the throng that followed the Saviour.

As Jesus passed the gate of Pilate's court, the cross which had been prepared for Barabbas was laid upon His bruised and bleeding shoulders. Two companions of Barabbas were to suffer death at the same time with Jesus, and upon them also crosses were placed. The Saviour's burden was too heavy for Him in His weak and suffering condition. Since the Passover supper with His disciples, He had taken neither food nor drink. He had agonized in the garden of Gethsemane in conflict with satanic agencies. He had endured the anguish of the betrayal, and had seen His disciples forsake Him and flee. He had been taken to Annas, then to Caiaphas, and then to Pilate. From Pilate He had been sent to Herod, then sent again to Pilate.

From insult to renewed insult, from mockery to mockery, twice tortured by the scourge,—all that night there had been scene after scene of a character to try the soul of man to the uttermost. Christ had not failed. He had spoken no word but that tended to glorify God. All through the disgraceful farce of a trial He had borne Himself with firmness and dignity. But when after the second scourging the cross was laid upon Him, human nature could bear no more. He fell fainting beneath the burden.

Bearing the Cross

The crowd that followed the Saviour saw His weak and staggering steps, but they manifested no compassion. They taunted and reviled Him because He could not carry the heavy cross. Again the burden was laid upon Him, and again He fell fainting to the ground. His persecutors saw that it was impossible for Him to carry His burden farther. They were puzzled to find anyone who would bear the humiliating load. The Jews themselves could not do this, because the defilement would prevent them from keeping the Passover. None even of the mob that followed Him would stoop to bear the cross.

At this time a stranger, Simon a Cyrenian, coming in from the country, meets the throng. He hears the taunts and ribaldry of the crowd; he hears the words contemptuously repeated, Make way for the King of the Jews! He stops in astonishment at the scene; and as he expresses his compassion, they seize him and place the cross upon his shoulders.

Simon had heard of Jesus. His sons were believers in the Saviour, but he himself was not a disciple. The bearing of the cross to Calvary was a blessing to Simon, and he was ever after grateful for this providence. It led him to take upon himself the cross of Christ from choice, and ever cheerfully stand beneath its burden.

Not a few women are in the crowd that follow the Uncondemned to His cruel death. Their attention is fixed upon Jesus. Some of them have seen Him before. Some have carried to Him their sick and suffering ones. Some have themselves been healed. The story of the scenes that have taken place is related. They wonder at the hatred of the crowd toward Him for whom their own hearts are melting and ready to break.

And notwithstanding the action of the maddened throng, and the angry words of the priests and rulers, these women give expression to their sympathy. As Jesus falls fainting beneath the cross, they break forth into mournful wailing.

This was the only thing that attracted Christ's attention. Although full of suffering, while bearing the sins of the world, He was not indifferent to the expression of grief. He looked upon these women with tender compassion. They were not believers in Him; He knew that they were not lamenting Him as One sent from God, but were moved by feelings of human pity. He did not despise their sympathy, but it awakened in His heart a deeper sympathy for them. "Daughters of Jerusalem," He said, "weep not for Me, but weep for yourselves, and for your children." From the scene before Him, Christ looked forward to the time of Jerusalem's destruction. In that terrible scene, many of those who were now weeping for Him were to perish with their children.

From the fall of Jerusalem the thoughts of Jesus passed to a wider Judgment. In the destruction of the impenitent city He saw a symbol of the final destruction to come upon the world. He said, "Then shall they begin to say to the mountains, Fall on us; and to the hills, Cover us. For if they do these things in a green tree, what shall be done in the dry?" By the green tree, Jesus represented Himself, the innocent Redeemer. God suffered His wrath against transgression to fall on His beloved Son. Jesus was to be crucified for the sins of men. What suffering, then, would the sinner bear who continued in sin? All the impenitent and unbelieving would know a sorrow and misery that language would fail to express.

Of the multitude that followed the Saviour to Calvary, many had attended Him with joyful hosannas and the waving of palm branches as He rode triumphantly into Jerusalem. But not a few who had then shouted His praise, because it was popular to do so, now swelled the cry of "Crucify Him, crucify Him." When Christ rode into Jerusalem, the hopes of the disciples had been raised to the highest pitch. They had pressed close about their Master, feeling that it was a high honor to be connected with Him. Now in His humiliation they followed Him at a distance. They were filled with grief, and bowed down with disappointed hopes. How were the words of Jesus verified: "All ye shall be offended because of Me this night: for it is written, I will smite the Shepherd, and the sheep of the flock shall be scattered abroad." Matthew 26:31.

The Place of Execution

Arriving at the place of execution, the prisoners were bound to the instruments of torture. The two thieves wrestled in the hands of those who placed them on the cross; but Jesus made no resistance.

The mother of Jesus, supported by John the beloved disciple, had followed the steps of her Son to Calvary. She had seen Him fainting under the burden of the cross, and had longed to place a supporting hand beneath His wounded head, and to bathe that brow which had once been pillowed upon her bosom. But she was not permitted this mournful privilege. With the disciples she still cherished the hope that Jesus would manifest His power, and deliver Himself from His enemies. Again her heart would sink as she recalled the words in which He had foretold the very scenes that were then taking place.

As the thieves were bound to the cross, she looked on with agonizing suspense. Would He Who had given life to the dead suffer Himself to be crucified? Would the Son of God suffer Himself to be thus cruelly slain? Must she give up her faith that Jesus was the Messiah? Must she witness His shame and sorrow, without even the privilege of ministering to Him in His distress? She saw His hands stretched upon the cross; the hammer and the nails were brought, and as the spikes were driven through the tender flesh, the heart-stricken disciples bore away from the cruel scene the fainting form of the mother of Jesus.

The Saviour made no murmur of complaint. His face remained calm and serene, but great drops of sweat stood upon His brow. There was no pitying hand to wipe the death dew from His face, nor words of sympathy and unchanging fidelity to stay His human heart.

While the soldiers were doing their fearful work, Jesus prayed for His enemies, "Father, forgive them; for they know not what they do." His mind passed from His Own suffering to the sin of His persecutors, and the terrible retribution that would be theirs. No curses were called down upon the soldiers who were handling Him so roughly. No vengeance was invoked upon the priests and rulers, who were gloating over the accomplishment of their purpose. Christ pitied them in their ignorance and guilt. He breathed only a plea for their forgiveness,—"for they know not what they do."

Had they known that they were putting to torture One Who had come to save the sinful race from eternal ruin, they would have been seized with remorse and horror. But their ignorance did not remove their guilt; for it was their privilege to know and accept Jesus as their Saviour. Some of them would yet see their sin, and repent, and be converted. Some by their impenitence would make it an impossibility for the prayer of Christ to be answered for them. Yet, just the same, God's purpose was reaching its fulfillment. Jesus was earning the right to become the Advocate of men in the Father's presence.

That prayer of Christ for His enemies embraced the world. It took in every sinner that had lived or should live, from the beginning of the world to the end of time. Upon all rests the guilt of crucifying the Son of God. To all, forgiveness is freely offered. "Whosoever will" may have peace with God, and inherit eternal life.

As soon as Jesus was nailed to the cross, it was lifted by strong men, and with great violence thrust into the place prepared for it. This caused the most intense agony to the Son of God. Pilate then wrote an inscription in Hebrew, Greek, and Latin, and placed it upon the cross, above the head of Jesus. It read, "Jesus of Nazareth the King of the Jews." This inscription irritated the Jews. In Pilate's court they had cried, "Crucify Him." "We have no king but Cæsar." John 19:15. They had declared that whoever should acknowledge any other king was a traitor. Pilate wrote out the sentiment they had expressed. No offense was mentioned, except that Jesus was the King of the Jews.

The inscription was a virtual acknowledgment of the allegiance of the Jews to the Roman power. It declared that whoever might claim to be the King of Israel would be judged by them worthy of death. The priests had overreached themselves. When they were plotting the death of Christ, Caiaphas had declared it expedient that one Man should die to save the nation. Now their hypocrisy was revealed. In order to destroy Christ, they had been ready to sacrifice even their national existence.

The priests saw what they had done, and asked Pilate to change the inscription. They said, "Write not, The King of the Jews; but that He said, I am King of the Jews." But Pilate was angry with himself because of his former weakness, and he thoroughly despised the jealous and artful priests and rulers. He replied coldly, "What I have written I have written."

A higher Power than Pilate or the Jews had directed the placing of that inscription above the head of Jesus. In the providence of God it was to awaken thought, and investigation of the Scriptures. The place where Christ was crucified was near to the city. Thousands of people from all lands were then at Jerusalem, and the inscription declaring Jesus of Nazareth the Messiah would come to their notice. It was a living truth, transcribed by a hand that God had guided.

In the sufferings of Christ upon the cross prophecy was fulfilled. Centuries before the crucifixion, the Saviour had foretold the treatment He was to receive. He said, "Dogs have compassed Me: the assembly of the wicked have enclosed Me: they pierced My hands and My feet. I may tell all My bones: they look and stare upon Me. They part My garments among them, and cast lots upon My vesture." Psalm 22:16-18.

The prophecy concerning His garments was carried out without counsel or interference from the friends or the enemies of the Crucified One. To the soldiers who had placed Him upon the cross, His clothing was given. Christ heard the men's contention as they parted the garments among them. His tunic was woven throughout without seam, and they said, "Let us not rend it, but cast lots for it, whose it shall be."

In another prophecy the Saviour declared, "Reproach hath broken My heart; and I am full of heaviness: and I looked for some to take pity, but there was none; and for comforters, but I found none. They gave Me also gall for My meat; and in My thirst they gave Me vinegar to drink." Psalm 69:20, 21.

To those who suffered death by the cross, it was permitted to give a stupefying potion, to deaden the sense of pain. This was offered to Jesus; but when He had tasted it, He refused it. He would receive nothing that could becloud His mind. His faith must keep fast hold upon God. This was His only strength. To becloud His senses would give Satan an advantage.

Hours of Agony

The enemies of Jesus vented their rage upon Him as He hung upon the cross. Priests, rulers, and scribes joined with the mob in mocking the dying Saviour. At the baptism and at the transfiguration the voice of God had been heard proclaiming Christ as His Son. Again, just before Christ's betrayal, the Father had spoken, witnessing to His divinity. But now the voice from heaven was silent. No testimony in Christ's favor was heard. Alone He suffered abuse and mockery from wicked men.

"If Thou be the Son of God," they said, "come down from the cross." "Let Him save Himself, if He be Christ, the chosen of God." In the wilderness of temptation Satan had declared, "If Thou be the Son of God, command that these stones be made bread." "If Thou be the Son of God, cast Thyself down" from the pinnacle of the Temple. Matthew 4:3, 6. And Satan with his angels, in human form, was present at the cross. The archfiend and his hosts were cooperating with the priests and rulers. The teachers of the people had stimulated the ignorant mob to pronounce judgment against One upon Whom many of them had never looked, until urged to bear testimony against Him. Priests, rulers, Pharisees, and the hardened rabble were confederated together in a satanic frenzy. Religious rulers united with Satan and his angels. They were doing his bidding.

Jesus, suffering and dying, heard every word as the priests declared, "He saved others; Himself He cannot save. Let Christ the King of Israel descend now from the cross, that we may see and believe." Christ could have come down from the cross. But it is because He would not save Himself that the sinner has hope of pardon and favor with God.

In their mockery of the Saviour, the men who professed to be the expounders of prophecy were repeating the very words which Inspiration had foretold they would utter upon this occasion. Yet in their blindness they did not see that they were fulfilling the prophecy. Those who in derision uttered the words, "He trusted in God; let Him deliver Him now, if He will have Him: for He said, I am the Son of God," little thought that their testimony would sound down the ages.

But although spoken in mockery, these words led men to search the Scriptures as they had never done before. Wise men heard, searched, pondered, and prayed. There were those who never rested until, by comparing Scripture with Scripture, they saw the meaning of Christ's mission. Never before was there such a general knowledge of Jesus as when He hung upon the cross. Into the hearts of many who beheld the crucifixion scene, and who heard Christ's words, the light of truth was shining.

To Jesus in His agony on the cross there came one gleam of comfort. It was the prayer of the penitent thief. Both the men who were crucified with Jesus had at first railed upon Him; and one under his suffering only became more desperate and defiant. But not so with his companion. This man was not a hardened criminal; he had been led astray by evil associations, but he was less guilty than many of those who stood beside the cross reviling the Saviour. He had seen and heard Jesus, and had been convicted by His teaching, but he had been turned away from Him by the priests and rulers. Seeking to stifle conviction, he had plunged deeper and deeper into sin, until he was arrested, tried as a criminal, and condemned to die on the cross. In the judgment hall and on the way to Calvary he had been in company with Jesus. He had heard Pilate declare, "I find no fault in Him." John 19:4. He had marked His godlike bearing, and His pitying forgiveness of His tormentors. On the cross he sees the many great religionists shoot out the tongue with scorn, and ridicule the Lord Jesus. He sees the wagging heads. He hears the upbraiding speeches taken up by his companion in guilt: "If Thou be Christ, save Thyself and us." Among the passersby he hears many defending Jesus. He hears them repeat His words, and tell of His works. The conviction comes back to him that this is the Christ. Turning to his fellow criminal he says, "Dost not thou fear God, seeing thou art in the same condemnation?"

The dying thieves have no longer anything to fear from man. But upon one of them presses the conviction that there is a God to fear, a future to cause him to tremble. And now, all sin-polluted as it is, his life history is about to close. "And we indeed justly," he moans; "for we receive the due reward of our deeds: but this Man hath done nothing amiss."

There is no question now. There are no doubts, no reproaches. When condemned for his crime, the thief had become hopeless and despairing; but strange, tender thoughts now spring up. He calls to mind all he has heard of Jesus, how He has healed the sick and pardoned sin. He has heard the words of those who believed in Jesus and followed Him weeping. He has seen and read the title above the Saviour's head. He has heard the passersby repeat it, some with grieved, quivering lips, others with jesting and mockery.

The Holy Spirit illuminates his mind, and little by little the chain of evidence is joined together. In Jesus, bruised, mocked, and hanging upon the cross, he sees the Lamb of God, That taketh away the sin of the world. Hope is mingled with anguish in his voice as the helpless, dying soul casts himself upon a dying Saviour. "Lord, remember me," he cries, "when Thou comest into Thy kingdom."

Quickly the answer came. Soft and melodious the tone, full of love, compassion, and power the words: Verily I say unto thee today, Thou shalt be with Me in Paradise.

For long hours of agony, reviling and mockery have fallen upon the ears of Jesus. As He hangs upon the cross, there floats up to Him still the sound of jeers and curses. With longing heart He has listened for some expression of faith from His disciples. He has heard only the mournful words, "We trusted that it had been He Which should have redeemed Israel." How grateful then to the Saviour was the utterance of faith and love from the dying thief!

While the leading Jews deny Him, and even the disciples doubt His divinity, the poor thief, upon the brink of eternity, calls Jesus Lord. Many were ready to call Him Lord when He wrought miracles, and after He had risen from the grave; but none acknowledged Him as He hung dying upon the cross save the penitent thief who was saved at the eleventh hour.

The bystanders caught the words as the thief called Jesus Lord. The tone of the repentant man arrested their attention. Those who at the foot of the cross had been quarreling over Christ's garments, and casting lots upon His vesture, stopped to listen. Their angry tones were hushed. With bated breath they looked upon Christ, and waited for the response from those dying lips.

As He spoke the words of promise, the dark cloud that seemed to enshroud the cross was pierced by a bright and living light. To the penitent thief came the perfect peace of acceptance with God. Christ in His humiliation was glorified. He Who in all other eyes appeared to be conquered was a Conqueror. He was acknowledged as the Sin Bearer. Men may exercise power over His human body. They may pierce the holy temples with the crown of thorns. They may strip from Him His raiment, and quarrel over its division. But they cannot rob Him of His power to forgive sins. In dying He bears testimony to His own divinity and to the glory of the Father. His ear is not heavy that it cannot hear, neither His arm shortened that it cannot save. It is His royal right to save unto the uttermost all who come unto God by Him.

I say unto thee today, Thou shalt be with Me in Paradise. Christ did not promise that the thief should be with Him in Paradise that day. He Himself did not go that day to Paradise. He slept in the tomb, and on the morning of the resurrection He said, "I am not yet ascended to My Father." John 20:17. But on the day of the crucifixion, the day of apparent defeat and darkness, the promise was given. "Today" while dying upon the cross as a malefactor, Christ assures the poor sinner, Thou shalt be with Me in Paradise.

The thieves crucified with Jesus were placed "on either side one, and Jesus in the midst." This was done by the direction of the priests and rulers. Christ's position between the thieves was to indicate that He was the greatest criminal of the three. Thus was fulfilled the Scripture, "He was numbered with the transgressors." Isaiah 53:12. But the full meaning of their act the priests did not see. As Jesus, crucified with the thieves, was placed "in the midst," so His cross was placed in the midst of a world lying in sin. And the words of pardon spoken to the penitent thief kindled a light that will shine to the earth's remotest bounds.

Amazing Love

With amazement the angels beheld *the infinite love of Jesus*, Who, suffering the most intense agony of mind and body, thought only of others, and encouraged the penitent soul to believe. In His humiliation He as a Prophet had addressed the daughters of Jerusalem; as Priest and Advocate He had pleaded with the Father to forgive His murderers; as a loving Saviour He had forgiven the sins of the penitent thief.

As the eyes of Jesus wandered over the multitude about Him,

one figure arrested His attention. At the foot of the cross stood His mother, supported by the disciple John. She could not endure to remain away from her Son; and John, knowing that the end was near, had brought her again to the cross. In His dying hour, Christ remembered His mother. Looking into her grief-stricken face and then upon John, He said to her, "Woman, behold thy son!" then to John, "Behold thy mother!" John understood Christ's words, and accepted the trust. He at once took Mary to his home, and from that hour cared for her tenderly.

O pitiful, loving Saviour; amid all His physical pain and mental anguish, He had a thoughtful care for His mother! He had no money with which to provide for her comfort; but He was enshrined in the heart of John, and He gave His mother to him as a precious legacy. Thus He provided for her that which she most needed,—the tender sympathy of one who loved her because she loved Jesus. And in receiving her as a sacred trust, John was receiving a great blessing. She was a constant reminder of his beloved Master.

The perfect example of Christ's filial love shines forth with undimmed luster from the mist of ages. For nearly thirty years Jesus by His daily toil had helped bear the burdens of the home. And now, even in His last agony, He remembers to provide for His sorrowing, widowed mother. The same spirit will be seen in every disciple of our Lord. Those who follow Christ will feel that it is a part of their religion to respect and provide for their parents. From the heart where His love is cherished, father and mother will never fail of receiving thoughtful care and tender sympathy.

And now the Lord of glory was dying, a ransom for the race. In yielding up His precious life, Christ was not upheld by triumphant joy. All was oppressive gloom. It was not the dread of death that weighed upon Him. It was not the pain and ignominy of the cross that caused His inexpressible agony. Christ was the Prince of sufferers; but His suffering was from a sense of the malignity of sin, a knowledge that through familiarity with evil, man had become blinded to its enormity. Christ saw how deep is the hold of sin upon the human heart, how few would be willing to break from its power. He knew that without help from God, humanity must perish, and He saw multitudes perishing within reach of abundant help.

Upon Christ as our Substitute and Surety was laid the iniquity of us all. He was counted a transgressor, that He might redeem us from the condemnation of the Law. The guilt of every descendant of Adam was pressing upon His heart. The wrath of God against sin, the terrible manifestation of His displeasure because of iniquity, filled the soul of His Son with consternation.

All His life Christ had been publishing to a fallen world the good news of the Father's mercy and pardoning love. Salvation for the chief of sinners was His theme. But now with the terrible weight of guilt He bears, He cannot see the Father's reconciling face. The withdrawal of the divine countenance from the Saviour in this hour of supreme anguish pierced His heart with a sorrow that can never be fully understood by man. So great was this agony that His physical pain was hardly felt.

Satan with his fierce temptations wrung the heart of Jesus. The Saviour could not see through the portals of the tomb. Hope did not present to Him His coming forth from the grave a conqueror, or tell Him of the Father's acceptance of the sacrifice. He feared that sin was so offensive to God that Their separation was to be eternal. Christ felt the anguish which the sinner will feel when mercy shall no longer plead for the guilty race. It was the sense of sin, bringing the Father's wrath upon Him as man's substitute, that made the cup He drank so bitter, and broke the heart of the Son of God.

Moment of Darkness

With amazement angels witnessed the Saviour's despairing agony. The hosts of Heaven veiled their faces from the fearful sight. Inanimate nature expressed sympathy with its insulted and dying Author. The sun refused to look upon the awful scene. Its full, bright rays were illuminating the earth at midday, when suddenly it seemed to be blotted out. Complete darkness, like a funeral pall, enveloped the cross. "There was darkness over all the land unto the ninth hour." There was no eclipse or other natural cause for this darkness, which was as deep as midnight without moon or stars. It was a miraculous testimony given by God that the faith of after generations might be confirmed.

In that thick darkness God's presence was hidden. He makes darkness His pavilion, and conceals His glory from human eyes. God and His holy angels were beside the cross. The Father was with His Son. Yet His presence was not revealed. Had His glory flashed forth from the cloud, every human beholder would have been destroyed. And in that dreadful hour Christ was not to be comforted with the Father's presence. He trod the winepress alone, and of the people there was none with Him.

In the thick darkness, God veiled the last human agony of His Son. All who had seen Christ in His suffering had been convicted of His divinity. That face, once beheld by humanity, was never forgotten. As the face of Cain expressed his guilt as a murderer, so the face of Christ revealed innocence, serenity, benevolence,—the image of God. But His accusers would not give heed to the signet of Heaven. Through long hours of agony Christ had been gazed upon by the jeering multitude. Now He was mercifully hidden by the mantle of God.

The silence of the grave seemed to have fallen upon Calvary. A nameless terror held the throng that was gathered about the cross. The cursing and reviling ceased in the midst of half-uttered sentences. Men, women, and children fell prostrate upon the earth. Vivid lightnings occasionally flashed forth from the cloud, and revealed the cross and the crucified Redeemer. Priests, rulers, scribes, executioners, and the mob, all thought that their time of retribution had come. After a while some whispered that Jesus would now come down from the cross. Some attempted to grope their way back to the city, beating their breasts and wailing in fear.

At the ninth hour the darkness lifted from the people, but still enveloped the Saviour. It was a symbol of the agony and horror that weighed upon His heart. No eye could pierce the gloom that surrounded the cross, and none could penetrate the deeper gloom that enshrouded the suffering soul of Christ. The angry lightnings seemed to be hurled at Him as He hung upon the cross. Then "Jesus cried with a loud voice, saying, Eloi, Eloi, lama sabachthani?" "My God, My God, why hast Thou forsaken Me?" As the outer gloom settled about the Saviour, many voices exclaimed: The vengeance of Heaven is upon Him. The bolts of God's wrath are hurled at Him, because He claimed to be the Son of God. Many who believed on

Him heard His despairing cry. Hope left them. If God had forsaken Jesus, in what could His followers trust?

When the darkness lifted from the oppressed spirit of Christ, He revived to a sense of physical suffering, and said, "I thirst." One of the Roman soldiers, touched with pity as he looked at the parched lips, took a sponge on a stalk of hyssop, and dipping it in a vessel of vinegar, offered it to Jesus.

But the priests mocked at His agony. When darkness covered the earth, they had been filled with fear; as their terror abated, the dread returned that Jesus would yet escape them. His words, "Eloi, Eloi, lama sabachthani?" they had misinterpreted. With bitter contempt and scorn they said, "This Man calleth for Elias." The last opportunity to relieve His sufferings they refused. "Let be," they said, "let us see whether Elias will come to save Him."

The spotless Son of God hung upon the cross, His flesh lacerated with stripes; those hands so often reached out in blessing, nailed to the wooden bars; those feet so tireless on ministries of love, spiked to the tree; that royal head pierced by the crown of thorns; those quivering lips shaped to the cry of woe.

And all that He endured—the blood drops that flowed from His head, His hands, His feet, the agony that racked His frame, and the unutterable anguish that filled His soul at the hiding of His Father's face—speaks to each child of humanity, declaring, It is for thee that the Son of God consents to bear this burden of guilt; for thee He spoils the domain of death, and opens the gates of Paradise. He Who stilled the angry waves and walked the foam-capped billows, Who made devils tremble and disease flee, Who opened blind eyes and called forth the dead to life,—offers Himself upon the cross as a Sacrifice, and this from love to thee. He, the Sin Bearer, endures the wrath of divine justice, and for thy sake becomes sin itself.

"It Is Finished"

In silence the beholders watched for the end of the fearful scene. The sun shone forth; but the cross was still enveloped in darkness. Priests and rulers looked toward Jerusalem; and lo, the dense cloud had settled over the city and the plains of Judea. The Sun of Righteousness, the Light of the world, was withdrawing His beams from the once favored city of Jerusalem. The fierce lightnings of God's wrath were directed against the fated city.

Suddenly the gloom lifted from the cross, and in clear, trumpet-like tones, that seemed to resound throughout creation, Jesus cried, "It is finished." "Father, into Thy hands I commend My spirit." A light encircled the cross, and the face of the Saviour shone with a glory like the sun. He then bowed His head upon His breast, and died.

Amid the awful darkness, apparently forsaken of God, Christ had drained the last dregs in the cup of human woe. In those dreadful hours He had relied upon the evidence of His Father's acceptance heretofore given Him. He was acquainted with the character of His Father; He understood His justice, His mercy, and His great love. By faith He rested in Him Whom it had ever been His joy to obey. And as in submission He committed Himself to God, the sense of the loss of His Father's favor was withdrawn. By faith, Christ was Victor.

Never before had the earth witnessed such a scene. The multitude stood paralyzed, and with bated breath gazed upon the Saviour. Again darkness settled upon the earth, and a hoarse rumbling, like heavy thunder, was heard. There was a violent earthquake. The people were shaken together in heaps. The wildest confusion and consternation ensued. In the surrounding mountains, rocks were rent asunder, and went crashing down into the plains. Sepulchers were broken open, and the dead were cast out of their tombs. Creation seemed to be shivering to atoms. Priests, rulers, soldiers, executioners, and people, mute with terror, lay prostrate upon the ground.

When the loud cry, "It is finished," came from the lips of Christ, the priests were officiating in the Temple. It was the hour of the evening sacrifice. The lamb representing Christ had been brought to be slain. Clothed in his significant and beautiful dress, the priest stood with lifted knife, as did Abraham when he was about to slay his son. With intense interest the people were looking on. But the earth trembles and quakes; for the Lord Himself draws near. With a rending noise the inner veil of the Temple is torn from top to bottom by an unseen hand, throwing open to the gaze of the multitude a place once filled with the presence of God. In this place the Shekinah had dwelt. Here God had manifested His glory above the mercy seat. No one but the high priest ever lifted the veil separating this apartment from the rest of the Temple. He entered in once a year to make an atonement for the sins of the people. But lo, this veil is rent in twain. The Most Holy Place of the earthly sanctuary is no longer sacred.

All is terror and confusion. The priest is about to slay the victim; but the knife drops from his nerveless hand, and the lamb escapes. Type has met Antitype in the death of God's Son. The great sacrifice has been made. The way into the Holiest is laid open. A new and living way is prepared for all. No longer need sinful, sorrowing humanity await the coming of the high priest. Henceforth the Saviour was to officiate as Priest and Advocate in the Heaven of heavens. It was as if a living voice had spoken to the worshipers: There is now an end to all sacrifices and offerings for sin. The Son of God is come according to His word, "Lo, I come (in the volume of the Book it is written of Me,) to do Thy will, O God." "By His Own blood" He entereth "in once into the holy place, having obtained eternal redemption for us." Hebrews 10:7; 9:12.

The Heart of Infinite Love[4]

It was to redeem us that Jesus lived and suffered and died. He became "a Man of Sorrows," that we might be made partakers of everlasting joy. God permitted His beloved Son, full of grace and truth, to come from a world of indescribable glory, to a world marred and blighted with sin, darkened with the shadow of death and the curse. He permitted Him to leave the bosom of His love, the adoration of the angels, to suffer shame, insult, humiliation, hatred, and death. "The chastisement of our peace was upon Him; and with His stripes we are healed." Isaiah 53:5.

Behold Him in the wilderness, in Gethsemane, upon the cross! The spotless Son of God took upon Himself the burden of sin. He Who had been one with God, felt in His soul the awful separation that sin makes between God and man. This wrung from His lips the anguished cry, "My God, My God, why hast Thou forsaken Me?" Matthew 27:46. It was the burden of sin, the sense of its terrible enormity, of its separation of the soul from God—it was this that broke the heart of the Son of God.

But this great sacrifice was not made in order to create in the Father's heart a love for man, not to make Him willing to save. No, no! "God so loved the world, that He gave His Only-Begotten Son." John 3:16. The Father loves us, not because of the great propitiation, but He provided the propitiation because He loves us. Christ was the medium through which He could pour out His infinite love upon a fallen world. "God was in Christ, reconciling the world unto Himself." 2 Corinthians 5:19. God suffered with His Son. In the agony of Gethsemane, the death of *Calvary, the heart of Infinite Love paid the price of our redemption.*

Jesus said, "Therefore doth My Father love Me, because I lay down My life, that I might take it again." John 10:17. That is, "My Father has so loved you that He even loves Me more for giving My life to redeem you. In becoming your Substitute and Surety, by surrendering My life, by taking your liabilities, your transgressions, I am endeared to My Father; for by My sacrifice, God can be just, and yet the Justifier of him who believeth in Jesus."

None but the Son of God could accomplish our redemption; for only He Who was in the bosom of the Father could declare Him. Only He Who knew the height and depth of the love of God could make it manifest. Nothing less than the infinite sacrifice made by Christ in behalf of fallen man could express the Father's love to lost humanity.

"God so loved the world, that He gave His Only-Begotten Son." He gave Him not only to live among men, to bear their sins, and die their Sacrifice. He gave Him to the fallen race. Christ was to identify Himself with the interests and needs of humanity. He Who was One with God has linked Himself with the children of men by ties that are never to be broken. Jesus is "not ashamed to call them brethren" (Hebrews 2:11); He is our Sacrifice, our Advocate, our Brother, bearing our human form before the Father's throne, and through eternal ages one with the race He has redeemed—the Son of Man. And all this that man might be uplifted from the ruin and degradation of sin that he might reflect the love of God and share the joy of holiness.

The price paid for our redemption, the infinite sacrifice of our Heavenly Father in giving His Son to die for us, should give us exalted conceptions of what we may become through Christ. As the inspired apostle John beheld the height, the depth, the breadth of the Father's love toward the perishing race, he was filled with adoration and reverence; and, failing to find suitable language in which to express the greatness and tenderness of this love, he called upon the world to behold it. "Behold, what manner of love the Father hath bestowed upon us, that we should be called the sons of God." 1 John 3:1.

What a value this places upon man! Through transgression the sons of man become subjects of Satan. Through faith in the atoning sacrifice of Christ the sons of Adam may become the sons of God. By assuming human nature, Christ elevates humanity. Fallen men are placed where, through connection with Christ, they may indeed become worthy of the name "sons of God."

Such love is without a parallel. Children of the heavenly King! Precious promise! Theme for the most profound meditation! *The matchless love of God* for a world that did not love Him! The thought has a subduing power upon the soul and brings the mind into captivity to the will of God. The more we study the divine character in the light of the cross, the more we see mercy, tenderness, and forgiveness blended with equity and justice, and the more clearly we discern innumerable evidences of a love that is infinite and a tender pity surpassing a mother's yearning sympathy for her wayward child.

~~~~~

"Christ was treated as we deserve, that we might be treated as He deserves. He was condemned for our sins, in which He had no share, that we might be justified by His righteousness, in which we had no share. He suffered the death which was ours, that we might receive the life which was His. 'With His stripes we are healed'" (Ellen G. White, *The Desire of Ages*, p. 25).
~~~~~

Notes:

1. Ellen G. White (1827–1915) was a woman of remarkable spiritual gifts who lived most of her life during the nineteenth century, yet through her writings and public ministry, she continues to make a revolutionary impact on millions of people around the world. She was a prolific Christian author. Unfortunately, it is only now that some are discovering this exceptionally insightful devotional writer. With the exception of the Bible writers, Ellen G. White is possibly the most translated author of all time. She is the most translated woman writer in the entire history of literature and the most translated American author of either gender. Although her formal schooling ended at age 9, her literary productions totaled more than 100,000 pages, or the equivalent of 25 million words. They deal with a wide range of practical subjects—spirituality, theology, education, health, family, etc. Massive amounts of these materials are preserved as letters, diaries, interviews, sermons, general manuscripts, periodical articles, pamphlets, and published books. Her published literary output during her lifetime included more than 5,000 periodical articles and 49 books. Today, including compilations from her manuscripts, more than 100 titles are available in English. But she was more than a prolific author. While the world is only now coming to appreciate her deep spiritual and practical insights on health, education, family, biblical spirituality, etc., millions have long recognized her as a recipient of the true gift of prophecy. Guided by the Holy Spirit, she exalted Jesus as humanity's only Saviour and pointed to Scripture as the sole basis for faith and practice. Her life-changing masterpiece on successful Christian living, *Steps to Christ*, has been published in about 150 languages, with well over 100 million copies in circulation. Her crowning literary achievement is the five-volume "Conflict of the Ages" series. Also known as the "Bible Study Companion Set," this work is one of the most spiritually uplifting studies on the Bible ever produced. It traces the conflict between good and evil from its origin to its dramatic, soon-to-unfold conclusion. A selection of Ellen G. White's best-known books is available to read online at: http://www.whiteestate.org/books/books.asp. In the "Recommended Reading" section of this present volume (see p. 213), you will find additional information on how to obtain printed copies of her major works.

2. Ellen G. White, *The Desire of Ages* (Boise, Idaho: Pacific Press, 1940), pp. 741-757. First published in 1898, the entire book is available to read online at http://www.whiteestate.org/books/da/da.asp.

3. Ibid. Notice that in the original work, there were no subheadings. For ease of reading, I have inserted the current subheadings to the original text. Also, as is characteristic of many nineteenth-century published works, some of the paragraphs in the original text were

quite long. In the selection cited here, I have divided such long paragraphs in more than a dozen places. But the text itself has been preserved as first published by the author in 1898, except for an occasional emphasis of my own and minor changes in spelling.

4. Ellen G. White, *Steps to Christ* (first published in 1892), pp. 13-15. The entire book is available to read online at http://www.whiteestate.org/books/sc/sc.asp. Again, the text itself has been preserved as first published by the author in 1892, except for an occasional emphasis of my own and minor changes in spelling.

16

Lyrics of Love

"To love a person is to learn the song that is in their heart, and to sing it to them when they have forgotten."
~Anonymous~

Love songs are always popular. How else do we explain the success of most pop singers? Turn on the radio, and you are likely to hear love songs. The lyrics are captivating, often in well-crafted poetry expressing deep human emotions or thoughts. Love poems, often set to music, are vehicles for songs of new love, disappointed love, romantic love, grateful love, crazy love, wounded love, and songs of love describing different emotions.

Those who have experienced true love have often written some of the most beautiful love poems and songs about the person of their affection. This phenomenon of composing lyrics of love goes all the way back to Bible times and runs through Christian history.

This chapter calls attention to some love gems that far outshine today's popular lyrics of love—whether Christian or non-Christian. These love gems from the Bible and Christian history reveal the beauty of true love and how we can talk about it in a way that glorifies God.

The Greatest Love Song

Some people are surprised to discover an explicit love poem or love song in the Bible—complete with romantic lyrics. But the Song of Songs is exactly that—a poem about love. The phrase "Song of Songs" is a Hebrew superlative expression and means "the best song," "the greatest song," or "the loveliest of songs."[1]

In Scripture are many poems set to music—even books of songs. There are songs that celebrate Creation, songs that speak of victory, and songs of praise and thanksgiving. But the Song of Songs contains the most excellent of them all. The theme of this song is *love*. Solomon, the wisest man who ever lived, wrote this famous love song or love poem. Of his 3,000 proverbs and 1,005 songs,[2] the Song of Songs is the best of all.

This love poem makes no direct references to God, prayer, worship, or piety. Unlike some other books of the Bible, this book is not introduced by a vision or any of the marks of immediate revelation and is never quoted in the New Testament. Yet it is the greatest love poem.

The transcendent excellence of Solomon's poem appears in the theme it addresses—love. The highlight of the Song of Songs is the intimate story of a man and a woman—their love, courtship, marriage, and undying mutual devotion. The book describes in intimate detail their feelings for each other and their longings to be together. In fact, immediately following the author's brief introduction in verse 1, the very next verse of the book records the prompting of the woman to her lover: "Let him kiss me with the kisses of his mouth"!

Because of the explicit romantic nature of this love poem (and also because it makes no references to the typical themes of religion or spirituality), over the years attempts have been made to exclude the Song of Songs from the canon of the Bible. For instance, in the sixteenth century, professor/theologian Fray Luis de León was dragged out of his classroom and imprisoned for four years. His only crime was that he translated the Song of Songs into Spanish!

Even though the Song of Songs contains the strongest argument for chastity before marriage, because of its explicit language on human sexuality, even ancient Hebrews forbade men from reading the Song of Songs until they were 30 years old!

But God has placed the Song of Songs in the Bible so we will understand the value that He Himself places upon the love of a man and a woman.

What is the meaning of this song? Much debate has occurred among Bible students over this question. Some say the Song of Songs is an allegory or a parable of God's love for His people, viewed either collectively or individually. Others think it is a literal story about married love—describing the intimate relation between King Solomon, the richest king ever to rule Israel, and his beloved bride, a poor country girl (identified simply as the Shulamite woman).

Personally, I believe it is both—a true historical account with dual applications. First, it teaches us about true love between man and woman, highlighting the joys and pains of love relationships and the beauty of romantic affections. Second, it teaches about God's boundless love for His people—both for His true church throughout the ages and for individual believers.

But regardless of how a person reads this love poem, Song of Songs teaches that there is nothing inherently wrong with love poems. Christians can write and read love poems, and even set them to music and sing them, provided they understand the spiritual purpose of such poems.

The Message of True Love Poems

The inspired love poem in the Bible sets a model for us regarding how the writing of love poems can be done truthfully and tastefully. Notice that unlike today's love songs, the poem in Song of Songs, though explicit, is never even slightly dirty or crude. Even when it describes sexual intimacy, it tastefully employs imagery from the world of nature. In this way, it does not insult the sensibility of readers.

The Song of Songs also explains what true love is and the boundaries God has set for its legitimate expression. For example, at the peak of their joy, the lovers repeatedly warn others not to stir up love prematurely: "Do not arouse or awaken love until it so desires" (2:7; 3:5; 8:4). Here is an exhortation to remain sexually pure before marriage. Thus, while affirming that God approves of and encourages sex within marriage, it also admonishes against sex outside of marriage.

The Song of Songs also recognizes the dangerously explosive side of love. "For love is as strong as death, its jealousy unyielding as the grave. It burns like blazing fire, like a mighty flame. Many waters cannot quench love; rivers cannot wash it away" (8:6, 7). The book seems to say, "Love is explosive—handle with care!"

This model love poem also affirms the preciousness of love: All a man's possessions cannot purchase it, nor (alternatively) should they be exchanged for it: "If one were to give all of his house for love, it would be utterly scorned" (8:7b).

Finally, the inspired poem also describes the exclusiveness of love: "My lover is mine, and I am his" (2:16). True love does not give license to infidelity, for it is committed and faithful to its original object of affection.

The love poem of the Song of Songs, then, presents the beauty of pure love between a man and a woman, which ripens into undying mutual devotion. Its basic message is the beauty, purity, and sacredness of love and marriage. At the same time, it should remind readers that behind all pure human love is the greatest, deepest love of all—the love of God. For God is love.

As we will demonstrate in the last chapter of this book, Song of Songs reveals the incomparable excellence of our loving Saviour, Jesus Christ. He is "the Chiefest among ten thousand," the One Who is "altogether lovely," our "Beloved" and "Friend" (5:10, 16).

Thus, every true love poem or love song describes God's love, which is the background and source of all true human love. Nowhere would one find as many true love songs or love poems as in the history of Christianity. Often, people who had experienced the love of Christ in their lives wrote these love songs or poems.

In the remainder of this chapter, I will call attention to a few love gems—poems or songs bequeathed to us from Christian history.

Compared to most of our contemporary love lyrics, these classical works stand apart in the powerful way they present the love of God. Millions can testify that these gems of Christian hymns have caused their hearts to love Christ more.

Familiar Love Songs

Christian hymns offer a rich source of love poems and love songs. Inasmuch as these hymns capture God's *agape* love, exemplified in the life and message of Jesus Christ, these classical songs have spoken to people of all ages and all nationalities. They have offered hope to the faint-hearted, rest to the weary, comfort to the afflicted, courage to the trembling, cheer to the despondent, power to the weak, and guidance or counsel to the perplexed during times of difficulty. Here are a few Christian love lyrics.[3]

Charles Wesley (1707–1788) is considered the "prince of English hymn writers" and "supreme poet of love to Jesus." Numerically surpassing even King David in output, Wesley penned some 8,989 poems—about a quarter of which were not sung. Of his 5,500 hymns, his song "Jesus, Lover of My Soul" is acclaimed by some as the greatest hymn ever written:

Jesus, lover of my soul,
Let me to Thy bosom fly,
While the billows near me roll,
While the tempest still is high.
Hide me, O my Saviour, hide!
Till the storm of life is past;
Safe into the haven guide,
O receive my soul at last!

Other refuge have I none,
Hangs my helpless soul on Thee;
Leave, O leave me not alone!
Still support and comfort me;
All my trust on Thee is stayed,

All my help from Thee I bring;
Cover my defenseless head
With the shadow of Thy wing.

Wilt Thou not regard my call?
Wilt Thou not accept my prayer?
Lo! I sink, I faint, I fall—
Lo! on Thee I cast my care;
Reach me out Thy gracious hand:
While I of Thy strength receive,
Hoping against hope I stand,
Dying, and behold, I live!

Thou, O Christ, art all I want,
More than all in Thee I find;
Raise the fallen, cheer the faint,
Heal the sick, and lead the blind.
Just and holy is Thy name,
I am all unrighteousness;
Vile and full of sin I am;
Thou art full of truth and grace.

Plenteous grace with Thee is found—
Grace to pardon all my sin;
Let the healing streams abound,
Make and keep me pure within;
Thou of life the Fountain art,
Freely let me take of Thee;
Spring Thou up within my heart,
Rise to all eternity.

Bernard of Clairvaux (1091-1153) was a Roman Catholic monk and head of the monastery in Clairvaux, France. He lived during the Middle Ages—a period of history characterized by spiritual and moral darkness in the Church (hence the period is often referred to as "The Dark Ages"). In the sixteenth century Martin Luther wrote of Bernard that "he was the best monk that ever lived, whom I admire beyond all the rest put together." Bernard's hymn, "Jesus, the Very Thought of Thee" is one of the most well-loved Christian songs.

Jesus, the very thought of Thee
With sweetness fills the breast;
But sweeter far Thy face to see,
And in Thy presence rest.

No voice can sing,
No heart can frame,
Nor can the memory find
A sweeter sound than Jesus' name,
The Saviour of mankind.

O hope of every contrite heart!
O joy of all the meek,
To those who fall, how kind Thou art!
How good to those who seek!

But what to those who find? Ah! this
Nor tongue nor pen can show:
The love of Jesus—what it is,
None but His loved ones know.

Jesus, our only joy be Thou,
As Thou our prize wilt be;
In Thee be all our glory now,
And through eternity.

Frances (Fanny) Jane Crosby (1820-1915) was an American hymn writer and poetess who wrote over 8,000 hymns during her life. Blind from infancy, she began to write poems when eight years old. One time a preacher sympathetically remarked, "I think it is a great pity that the Master did not give you sight when He showered so many other gifts upon you." She replied quickly, "Do you know that if at birth I had been able to make one petition, it would have been that I should be born blind?" "Why?" asked the surprised clergyman. "Because when I get to heaven, the first face that shall ever gladden my sight will be that of my Saviour!" Fanny Crosby's song "Blessed Assurance, Jesus Is Mine!" has been a source of inspiration to millions around the world:

Blessed assurance, Jesus is mine!
O, what a foretaste of glory divine!
Heir of salvation, purchase of God,
Born of His Spirit, washed in His blood.

Refrain:
This is my story, this is my song,
Praising my Saviour all the day long;
This is my story, this is my song,
Praising my Saviour all the day long.

Perfect submission, perfect delight,
Visions of rapture now burst on my sight.
Angels descending bring from above
Echoes of mercy, whispers of love.

Refrain

Perfect submission, all is at rest,
I in my Saviour am happy and blest,
Watching and waiting, looking above,
Filled with His goodness, lost in His love.

Refrain

John Newton (1725-1807) was a very remarkable man. In his young days he lived a very wild, reckless, sinful life. But by the grace of God, he was converted and became one of the holiest of saints—the writer of many beautiful hymns. His song, "How Sweet the Name" describes Jesus as his Shepherd, Guardian, Friend, Prophet, Priest, King, Lord, Life, Way, and End. In this song Jesus guards, guides, keeps, and feeds us—finally receiving us to be with Him forever in glory.

How sweet the name of Jesus sounds
In a believer's ear!
It soothes his sorrows, heals his wounds,
And drives away his fear.

It makes the wounded spirit whole,
And calms the troubled breast;
'Tis manna to the hungry soul,
And to the weary, rest.

Dear name, the rock on which I build,
My shield, and hiding place,
My never-failing treasury, filled
With boundless stores of grace.

Jesus! my Shepherd, Guardian, Friend,
My Prophet, Priest, and King!
My Lord, my Life, my Way, my End!
Accept the praise I bring.

Weak is the effort of my heart,
And cold my warmest thought;
But when I see Thee as Thou art,
I'll praise Thee as I ought.

Till then I would Thy love proclaim
With every fleeting breath;
And may the music of Thy name
Refresh my soul in death!

Will Lamartine Thompson (1847-1909), a native of East Liverpool, Ohio, was both a lyricist and a composer. To ensure that he would always remember words or melodies that came to him at odd times, he said: "No matter where I am, at home or hotel, at the store or traveling, if an idea or theme comes to me that I deem worthy of a song, I jot it down in verse. In this way I never lose it." Thompson's hymn "Jesus Is All The World to Me" explains why Christ should be the focal point of our lives:

Jesus is all the world to me, my life, my joy, my all;
He is my strength from day to day, without Him I would fall.
When I am sad to Him I go, no other one can cheer me so;
When I am sad, He makes me glad, He's my Friend.

Jesus is all the world to me, my Friend in trials sore;
I go to Him for blessings, and He gives them o'er and o'er.
He sends the sunshine and the rain, He
sends the harvest's golden grain;
Sunshine and rain, harvest of grain, He's my Friend.

Jesus is all the world to me, and true to Him I'll be;
O how could I this Friend deny, when He's so true to me?
Following Him I know I'm right, He watches o'er me day and night;
Following Him by day and night, He's my Friend.

Jesus is all the world to me, I want no better Friend;
I trust Him now, I'll trust Him when life's fleeting days shall end.
Beautiful life with such a Friend; beautiful life that has no end,
Eternal life, eternal joy, He's my Friend.

James Grindlay Small (1817-1888) wrote the song "I've Found a Friend" to capture God's enduring love for His children. This song weaves together a number of Bible passages. From Solomon we learn that God is our loving Friend: "Yea, He is altogether lovely. This is my Beloved, and this is my Friend" (Song of Songs 5:16). Through the prophet Hosea, we discover how He draws His children with cords of love: "I drew them with gentle cords, with bands of love" (Hosea 11:4). And the apostle Paul describes the strength of God's cords of love: "For I am persuaded, that neither death, nor life, nor angels, nor principalities, nor powers, nor things present, nor things to come, nor height, nor depth, nor any other creature, shall be able to separate us from the love of God, which is in Christ Jesus our Lord" (Romans 8:38, 39).

Proof of Love

I've found a Friend; oh, such a Friend!
He loved me ere I knew Him;
He drew me with the cords of love,
And thus He bound me to Him.
And 'round my heart still closely twine
Those ties which nought can sever,
For I am His, and He is mine,
Forever and forever.

I've found a Friend; oh, such a Friend!
He bled, He died to save me;
And not alone the gift of life,
But His own self He gave me.
Nought that I have my own I call,
I hold it for the Giver;
My heart, my strength, my life, my all,
Are His, and His forever.

I've found a Friend; oh, such a Friend!
All power to Him is given;
To guard me on my upward course,
And bring me safe to Heaven.
The eternal glories gleam afar,
To nerve my faint endeavor;
So now to watch, to work, to war,
And then to rest forever.

I've found a Friend; oh, such a Friend!
So kind, and true, and tender,
So wise a Counselor and Guide,
So mighty a Defender.
From Him, Who loveth me so well,
What power my soul can sever?
Shall life or death, or Earth, or Hell?
No; I am His forever.

The above examples of Christian hymns testify to the power of biblically grounded love lyrics. They have power to lift the human spirit above earthly cares and trials. They are able to disperse the clouds of doubt and fear. But more important, because they are rooted in praise and prayer, trust and love, faith and hope, and similar sentiments, these gems of Christian love lyrics have power to lead souls to Him who is the Source, embodiment, and Model of genuine Love—Jesus Christ, our Lord.

Notes:

1. The Hebrew superlative expression for this love song (the "Song of Songs") is similar to biblical expressions such as "God of gods," "Lord of lords," "King of kings," and "Holy of holies," each referring to the greatest God, Lord, King, or "the most holy," respectively.
2. In 1 Kings 4:29, 32 we read: "God gave Solomon wisdom and very great insight, and a breadth of understanding as measureless as the sand on the seashore. . . . He spoke three thousand proverbs and his songs numbered a thousand and five."
3. The Cyber Hymnal website has over 6,200 Christian hymns and Gospel songs from many denominations. On this site, you'll find lyrics, scores, MIDI files or music, pictures, history, and more. See http://www.cyberhymnal.org/index.htm#lk.

PART V

LOVE THOUGHTS

17

Yearning for Love

"Love cures people—both the ones who give it and the ones who receive it."
~Karl Menninger~

Are you longing for love? Do you yearn to love or be loved? Deep down in your soul, is there an irresistible desire to be desired? Are you bursting to share something you have with someone?

Do you sense or feel a void in your life—a deep void that doesn't seem to be filled by things you currently have—such as pleasure, wealth, ease, fame, accomplishments, or power?

Are you longing to belong—perhaps because you're presently alone, lonely, or even in a relationship where you've never truly experienced genuine love? Have you been let down by previous relationships and affections, and do you desire something better?

Do you feel that you need a certain kind of security, protection, understanding, or companionship with someone with whom you can meaningfully spend your life together—for this life or for eternity?

Do you long for someone who will accept you as you are, yet bring out the best in you—someone who will go any distance *with* you and *for* you?

Do you need a true friend—someone you can talk to, someone who will be there for you at all times, and with whom you can do things together or with whom you can share thoughts?

Do you yearn for real intimacy—intimacy with someone you can actually call your own—one special person who can make your life complete?

If your answer to any of these questions is "Yes," then what you really need is *true* love. For,

Where There's Love . . .

There is a special Person
Who is beyond comparison,
And is the joy of every season.

You see, genuine love is not an abstraction or a concept. It is not just a feeling or mere sentimental or sensual passion. Love is a Person—that *one* special Person meant for you. The yearning in your heart is actually a desire for God Himself. For as explained in the preface to the book *The Desire of Ages*—the book we referred to in our discussion of "The Proof of Love"...

> In the hearts of all mankind, of whatever race or station in life, there are inexpressible longings for something they do not now possess. This longing is implanted in the very constitution of man by a merciful God, that man may not be satisfied with his present conditions or attainments, whether bad, or good, or better. God desires that the human shall seek the best, and find it to the eternal blessing of his soul.
>
> Satan, by wily scheme and craft, has perverted these longings of the human heart. He makes men believe that this desire may be satisfied by pleasure, by wealth, by ease, by fame, by power; but those who have been thus deceived by him (and they number myriads) find all these things pall upon the sense, leaving the soul as barren and unsatisfied as before.
>
> It is God's design that this longing of the human heart should lead to the One Who alone is able to satisfy it. The desire is

> *of* Him that it may lead *to* Him, the fullness and fulfillment of that desire. That fullness is found in Jesus the Christ, the Son of the Eternal God. "For it was the good pleasure of the Father that in Him should all the fullness dwell;" "for in Him dwelleth all the fullness of the Godhead bodily." And it is also true that "in Him ye are made full" with respect to every desire divinely implanted and normally followed.
>
> Haggai calls Him "The Desire of all nations," and we may well call Him "The Desire of all ages," even as He is "The King of ages."[1]

Indeed, Jesus is that special Person you and I need in our lives if we are to experience true love. He alone is the One Who can satisfy the deepest yearnings of the human heart. While here on Earth, Jesus revealed what true love is. For He was truly God, even as He was truly man. And the Holy Scripture says that God is love. None can therefore fully experience true love without having Jesus in their lives. To know Christ is to know Him as:

> The Fullness of the Godhead, the infinitely merciful Saviour of sinners, the Sun of Righteousness, the merciful High Priest, the Healer of all human maladies and diseases, the tender, compassionate Friend, the constant, ever-present and helpful Companion, the Prince of the House of David, the Shield of His people, the Prince of Peace, the Coming King, the Everlasting Father, the culmination and fruition of the desires and hopes of all ages.[2]

So then, if the longings and desires of your soul are not yet satisfied, and if you need to love or to be loved, the only way to fill this heart longing is to get to know Christ. He is the fruition of the desires and hopes of all ages. Only as you know Christ will you experience, in the words of the Bible, that "fullness of joy" and "pleasures for evermore," which will be the ripened fruitage of all those who find in Jesus the "all in all," "the Rose of Sharon," "the lily of the valleys," "the Chiefest among ten thousand," and the One "altogether lovely."[3]

The love you yearn for is, therefore, a longing for Jesus. Without Him, you will still feel the emptiness and ache in your heart. For,

None Can Live Without Love
It's the cure for hearts that starve
A *Personal* gift from our Father above
For "God is love"
1 John 4:8, 16

May our yearning for love lead us to the God Who is Love. And thus may we say with David, "As the deer pants for the water brooks, so pants my soul for You, O God" (Psalm 42:1).

Notes:

1. As mentioned in chapter 15 of this volume, millions judge *The Desire of Ages* (1898) to be the best devotional biography on Christ. The entire book is available online at http://www.whiteestate.org/books/da/da.asp.
2. Ibid.
3. Psalm 16:11; Ephesians 1:23; Song of Songs 2:1; 5:10, 16.

18

Passion of Love

"God loves each of us as if there were only one of us."
~St. Augustine~

It is the nature of love to be passionate. It has an intense, almost overpowering, interest in the object of its affection. Wrongly directed, the consequences of this passion can be devastating, even fatal. But rightly directed, love's passion brings true fulfillment, satisfaction, and joy.

Divine love has an irresistible interest in the well-being of the object of its affection. The supreme goal of God's love, manifested in Christ, is an abundant, unending quality of life for humanity. This fact is found in the Bible's best-known text: "For God so loved the world, that He gave His Only-Begotten Son, that whosoever believeth in Him *should not perish, but have everlasting life*" (John 3:16, emphasis added).

"Everlasting life" should not be understood as merely length but as *quality* of life—a life that, by its quality, knows itself to be deathless. The pursuit of any form of "love" outside its true divine source will result in unfulfillment and hurt. The only real, meaningful, lasting love is that which has its origin in God, through His Son, Jesus

Christ. And Christ is passionately determined to offer this love to anyone who is yearning for love.

Relentless Love

If there exists a yearning in the human heart for love, there is in Christ's heart a much greater yearning to love humanity. And whereas even the best or noblest of human love is tainted by the essential selfishness of our fallen humanity, Christ's all-consuming love is so pure and amazing that it defies adequate human explanation.

One of the most gripping descriptions of Christ's passionate love that I've read comes from a chapter in Ken McFarland's book, *John: Bridge to Space Island.* In it he describes the love of Jesus as "the Hound of Heaven," an expression that evokes the imagery of a well-trained dog (hound) pursuing its quarry with undeviating single-mindedness. The depiction in this book is so compelling that to take anything out of it is to diminish our understanding of Christ's determined love that will not give up on anyone.[1] Each of the following six elements of Christ's love enables us to understand the true nature of love's passion.

1. Love Is Determined

One Christian author entitled her book *His Stubborn Love.* Christ made us because He wanted us. He loved us when we were still just a thought in His mind. And when, because of sin, we fled Him, He pursued us, determined to win us back. He simply cannot do without us. You and I probably have little idea as to just how badly Christ wants to win us back. He will spare nothing—not the angels of Heaven, not the Holy Spirit, not His Own life—to appeal to us to come back to Him. He will be discouraged by nothing—a Devil, a cross, our indifference—in His efforts to win our love.

The Hound of Heaven is persistent, relentless, tenacious, *determined.* He won't give you up until either He has won your love or you have rejected Him entirely.

2. Love Cannot Be Quenched

Nothing you can do can make Christ stop loving you. Nothing.

You can ignore Him days without number. You can reject Him. You can deny that He exists. You can mock and ridicule and curse Him. You can claim His name but play the Devil's game. You can be ashamed of Him. You can hate Him bitterly. You can run away from Him. You can pledge your allegiance to His greatest enemy. You can squander on your own gratification all His gifts to you. You can defy Him. You can portray Him to others as severe and ruthless and uncaring. You can shut Him totally out of your life. You can blame Him for all the evil in your world. You can whip Him till He bleeds and spit on Him and nail Him to a cross and laugh while He dies of a broken heart.

You can do all this. But one thing you can never do. You can never make Him stop loving you. Never.

3. Love Takes the Initiative

Christ does not wait for us to fall in love with Him. "We love, because He first loved us" (1 John 4:19). "But God demonstrates His Own love for us in this: While we were still sinners, Christ died for us" (Romans 5:8).

No matter how far we run from Him, no matter how deeply we plunge into sin, no matter how helpless and hopeless we may feel, Christ comes looking for us. He is the Alpha and the Omega, the Beginning and the End, the Author and the Finisher of our faith.

The first step in our salvation, the first move to restore our broken relationship, the first decision that ultimately leads us back home—is His. It may seem to us that we went looking for Him. But if we did, it was in response to His prior initiative.

And that prior initiative, in every case, is the steady, constant drawing of His love. In this whole process, Christ acts—and we react. Christ loves. We respond.

> The sinner may resist this love, may refuse to be drawn to Christ; but if he does not resist he will be drawn to Jesus.—*Steps to Christ,* p. 27.

One veteran pastor preaches a sermon entitled "It's Hard to Be Lost, and Easy to Be Saved." Most of us have probably concluded much the opposite—that it's hard to be saved and all too easy to be lost. But if Christ takes the initiative in our salvation, and our part is simply to respond to that initiative of love—to not resist it—is it possible that salvation may not be so difficult after all?

I'm glad that the shepherd didn't wait for the one lost sheep to find its way back home but went out looking for it. I'm glad that the housewife didn't wait for the lost coin to move itself out into the open but swept the floor till she found it. I'm glad that the father's long-distance love followed the prodigal son to the far country and brought him home again. I'm glad that Christ didn't wait till I got my act together to die for me. And I'm glad that He doesn't wait for me to make the first move toward Him but sends His love after me to win me back—even as I turn my back on Him once more.[2]

4. Love Is Forever

Once Christ begins loving someone, He never stops. His love for you will never fail or fade. And I am convinced that if, ultimately, you reject His love and choose eternal oblivion rather than eternity in His presence, He will love you still.

And for all eternity there will be a great, aching void in His heart—a never-diminishing grief that you are not there. God will not take your loss philosophically, but personally. And the passing of eons will not find Him missing you any less.

For all His created beings who are finally lost, He once gave His life because He loved. He loved Cain. He loved Judas. He will love the last of the lost to be born on this earth. And I firmly believe that God never stops loving *anyone*. Even the final passing of Satan himself will bring inexpressible grief to the heart of Christ. He loved Lucifer.

And if His love is forever, what a tragedy if any of us should miss out on being its eternal recipients.

5. Love Is Enough

Every one of us wants to be loved. Every one of us *needs* to be loved. And for most of us, the great driving hunger of our lives—the overriding search for happiness that consumes us—is really an effort to find love.

If I'm beautiful, maybe you'll love me. If I'm good, maybe you'll love me. If I'm successful, maybe you'll love me. If I entertain you, maybe you'll love me. If I love *you*, maybe you'll love me. So we humans look constantly to one another to fill our need for love. But human love—while it can be intensely satisfying—never seems wholly adequate to meet the truly unremitting need we seem to have for love.

Many who lose possessions, friends, and every other earthly advantage find themselves with nothing left but the love of Christ—only to discover what is true for all of us: that His love is enough. Christ loves you with no strings. No ifs. No conditions. He loves you if you have nothing. He loves you if you are a failure. He loves you if you're ugly. He loves you no matter how far down you've fallen. He loves you—not for what you have or what you do—but for simply being you.

6. Love Is Personal

"God so loved the *world*," John wrote. But make no mistake about it. God did not send Christ to die for real estate. Though He made them, He is not enamored of skies and seas and rocks and trees. He is in love with *you*—and with me.

But doesn't He have over six billion other human beings on Earth to love? How personal can He really be?

While our daughter was an infant, I could not imagine being able to love any other child as much as I loved her. But then her brother arrived, and I was pleasantly surprised to learn that I loved our second fully as much as the first—and our first no less than before. Today, with our two children, I do not have to divide the love I originally felt for our first child two ways. And I don't love "the children" as a group—I love them personally, individually.[3]

I'm not sure I have the capacity to love six billion people, each in a personal way. But for God, that's no problem.

> The relations between God and each soul are as distinct and full as though there were not another soul upon the earth to share His watchcare, not another soul for whom He gave His beloved Son.—*Steps to Christ*, p. 100.

God has time for you, my friend. He's not too busy with running the universe or relating to other people to give you His full, undivided attention. He loves you supremely; and if it matters to you, it matters to Him.

I confess I can't begin to fathom such love. It's so enormous that it seems that even eternity will be too short to begin understanding it. But I'm everlastingly thankful that such love is there, because—oh, how much I need it!

What Manner of Love!

Such is the nature of the passion of true love. Christ's is persistent, relentless, tenacious, *determined.* It cannot be quenched—even if we spit into its face and nail it to the cross. It takes the initiative—even when we were sinners. It is forever—it will never fail or fade. It is enough—wholly adequate to meet all our needs, with no strings attached. And it is personal—as distinct and full as though you were the only person on this planet. "Behold what manner of love the Father has bestowed on us, that we should be called children of God!" (1 John 3:1).

We can manifest this kind of love to our loved ones only when we know God, the Source of true love. For to know Him is to love Him. And to love Him is to serve Him. And to serve Him is to love our fellow human beings with the same kind of holy passion.

Notes:

1. I'm indebted to Ken McFarland for his permission for me to include in this work a modified chapter of his book *John: Bridge to Space Island* (Boise: Pacific Press, 1986), pp. 43-48. This work consists of thirteen devotionals on selected themes from the Gospel of John. The book was produced as a supplement to a 1986 Adult Sabbath School Bible Study Guide, which Ken also authored. I've reproduced here a substantial por-

tion of one of his chapters, with only minor modifications in a few places. The unusual expression "Hound of Heaven" referred to comes from the classic poem by Francis Thompson (1859–1907): "The Hound of Heaven."

2. See Luke 15 for Christ's three parables: the lost sheep, the lost coin, and the lost son.

3. In this paragraph, I have personalized McFarland's family size to reflect the realities of my *own* family. Because Ken has four grown children, in his original essay, he wrote this paragraph as follows: "But then her sister arrived, and I was pleasantly surprised to learn that I loved my second fully as much as the first—and my first no less than before. Today, with four grown children, I do not have to divide the love I originally felt for my first child four ways. And I don't love 'the children' as a group—I love them personally, individually."

19

Experience of Love

"To love is to receive a glimpse of heaven."
~Karen Sunde~

Perhaps the most important of all questions ever posed in any meaningful relationship is: "Do you love me?" Simple as the question sounds, it is a profound one.

The question is especially heart-searching if it comes from a special person whose tender affections you desperately desire. Even more so, if—after you have betrayed the trust of this particular individual—the same person takes the initiative by coming back to you, takes you aside privately, and gently and graciously asks you, "Do you love me?"

In this kind of context, an affirmative response to the question can radically transform a person's life. For as we shall soon discover, the "Do you love me?" question expresses a longing desire either to kindle a nonexistent love relationship or to restore one that has been damaged.

In this chapter, we will attempt to answer this simple yet profound love question. Our discussion not only holds promise for those who have never experienced true love but also for those who have lost it, after having once experienced the joy and assurance of true love.

Question of Love

Some two thousand years ago, our Lord Jesus Christ posed a question to one of His disciples—a question that begs every human being for an honest answer. Three times Jesus asked the apostle Peter, "Simon son of John, Do you love Me?" (John 21:15-17).

Prior to this time, Peter had professed *great love* for the Lord. On the very night he would betray his Master he had even boasted, "Even if all fall away on account of You, I never will. . . . Even if I have to die with You, I will never disown You."[1] But Peter demonstrated *little love* for the Saviour when he slept in the garden—and *no love* for the Lord when he thrice denied Him in the high priest's palace.

It is therefore not without significance that, after His resurrection, when our Lord Jesus sought to restore a remorseful Peter to an intimate relationship with Himself, Jesus also thrice repeated the question, "Do you love Me?"

Notice some specific things about our Lord's question of love.

First, the question deals with the most important thing in the world: love. The probing question, "Do you *love* Me?" is not about anything else. Christ did not ask Peter, "Are you a religious person? Are you a Christian? Do you go to church? Do you know the doctrines?" He didn't even ask Peter how much he had sacrificed for the Lord, or whether he'd had any extraordinary or miraculous experiences.

I'm sure if the Lord had asked those other questions, Peter could easily have responded, "Yes, Lord, I am a very religious or spiritual person. I have sacrificed so much for You, for I have 'given up everything to follow You.'"[2] Peter could also have responded, "Indeed, I am a real Christian, for I confessed You publicly when I alone could correctly declare that 'You are the Christ, the Son of the living God.'"[3] And the apostle could even have easily replied, "Certainly, Lord, You know I am one of the most respected church officers, for You Yourself had ordained me as an apostle. Since then, I have walked on the sea, cast out devils, and witnessed and performed many other real miracles."

While all this was true of Peter and could be true of us, those were not the questions Christ asked. Our Lord's question had to do with love, without which all of the above professions, actions, and experiences are nothing.

Second, Christ's question, "Do you love *Me*?" concerns what ought to be *the* ultimate object of our affections—the Person of Jesus Christ. Is your heart set upon Me, and are you trusting in Me for all things, in every circumstance and season of your life? Or is your heart somewhere else—on other relationships, pleasure, wealth, power, accomplishments, appearance, etc.?

Third, Christ's question is personal: "Do *you* love Me?" Christ didn't ask about someone else's love. For no one else's love for Jesus—whether it is the love that your family members, friends, pastor, or church may have for Him—will be reckoned to your account as a substitute for your personal love for Jesus.

Finally, the question has to do with the present situation: "*Do* you love Me?"—not "*Did* you love Me?" Yesterday's profession of love will not do for today. I'm sure many of us can testify, all too painfully, of individuals who once passionately loved us, but today those very people have become our bitterest enemies.

Christ's question, "Do you love Me?" was the most important question Peter ever faced. Our Lord intended it to show Peter the difference between the kind of love he had for Christ and the kind of love Christ required of him. But more important, the question was calculated to effect a transformation in Peter's life.

As noted earlier, it remains the one question that demands an answer from every rational human being: "Do you love Jesus Christ?" The response we give will determine whether or not we can experience, rekindle, or restore the love we yearn for.

Let's now consider the context of this profound question of love and how it played out in Peter's encounter with Christ.

Context of Love

The last chapter of the Gospel of John—the chapter from which we get the account of Jesus' probing question to Peter—is a beautiful description of God's amazing grace in restoring people who have woefully failed the Lord or anyone else they dearly love. Scattered through this chapter are many hints of God's quiet grace and wooing love.

The events of John 21 took place a few days after the most significant event in Peter's life—his betrayal of Christ on the night of our Lord's trial. Worthy of note is that not only did Peter deny Christ, he did so on the same night when he had thrice boasted that he would die for Christ. Worse still, when confronted by a powerless servant girl, Peter denied ever having any relationship at all with Jesus. He emphatically protested, "I don't know the Man!"[4]

Several days then pass after Peter betrayed his Master. He is now by the Sea of Galilee, having invited some of the disciples of Christ to join him in fishing. The Sea of Galilee was where Peter first met Jesus. It was here that Peter "left everything and followed Him" (Luke 5:11).

Now the apostle is back in Galilee, feeling totally devastated and disappointed in himself. At this particular time after Christ's resurrection, Peter may have been feeling he was a spiritual failure, on account of his terrible conduct. He didn't feel he was worthy of Christ's love or Christ's work. He may have said to himself, "I can no longer be a 'fisher of men'—I'm disqualified. I'm going to be a fisher of real fish. After all, that's the only thing I know how to do well."

But what Peter may not have realized was that even before he left Judea for Galilee, Christ had determined to meet him there, having foreseen that Peter would abandon his calling and return to Galilee. And there the remorseful apostle would need the Saviour's touch of grace and love.

You may recall that shortly before His death, Jesus had told the disciples about His impending suffering and crucifixion and then added, "But after I am risen again, I will go before you into Galilee."[5] Also, on the resurrection day, the angel at Christ's tomb confirmed the appointment when he told the grieving women at the tomb, "Go your way, tell His disciples *and Peter* that He goeth before you into Galilee: there shall ye see Him, as He said unto you."[6]

That moment to "see" Jesus had finally arrived. Though Peter had at least twice seen the resurrected Jesus in Jerusalem, this appointment to "see" Christ in Galilee would be much different. Jesus would both transform and restore Peter at Galilee. But before doing so, He would first make the apostle discover what had led to his spiritual failure.

Thus, the account in John 21:4-14 reveals a dramatized recapitulation of many of the significant events in Christ's relationship with Peter during the three years they had been together.[7] It almost seems as if Jesus intentionally wanted Peter to recall their previous relationship and what they had been through together.

The timing of Christ's "Do you love Me?" question is also significant. It was *after* He had dined with Peter and the disciples. Because Christ foresaw that the love question He would ask Peter would be an agonizing one to the repentant apostle, He would not ask the question till they had first dined. Christ would not want to spoil Peter's dinner. By first dining with him, in the company of the other disciples, Jesus was assuring Peter that He still loved him just as much as He loved the other disciples.

The act of dining together was an act of reconciliation. It suggested to both Peter and the other disciples that Christ did not consider Peter a criminal but a friend. Peter was already beaten up by his sin and guilt. He had already felt unworthy even to be welcomed back into Christ's fold. Christ, therefore, wanted Peter to know that he was as dear to Him as ever. Here is Christ's *agape* love of tenderness and kindness at work.

Another significant detail to note is that after the meal, Christ takes Peter on a walk—just the two of them apart, privately. From verse 20 we gather that Peter and Christ were some distance away from the others. It was during this private walk that our Lord asked Peter that heart-searching question, "Do you love Me?" That question would lead the apostle to come to terms with true love.

Encounter With Love

The Bible records Peter's encounter with Christ in John 21:15-17 thus:

> When they had finished eating, Jesus said to Simon Peter, "Simon son of John, do you truly love Me more than these?"
>
> "Yes, Lord," he said, "You know that I love You."
>
> Jesus said, "Feed My lambs."
>
> Again Jesus said, "Simon son of John, do you truly love Me?"
>
> He answered, "Yes, Lord, You know that I love You."
>
> Jesus said, "Take care of My sheep."
>
> The third time He said to him, "Simon son of John, do you love Me?"
>
> Peter was hurt because Jesus asked him the third time, "Do you love Me?" He said, "Lord, You know all things; You know that I love You."

A couple of observations are worth noting in the above biblical account.

First, notice the name by which our Lord addresses the apostle. Christ does not call him Cephas or Peter—the names He had previously given him (for Peter had lost the confidence of others in his strength and stability, which those names signified). Instead, Christ calls the apostle by his original name, Simon.

The use of his original name was designed to affect Peter experientially, pointing the apostle back to the three times in the past when Christ touched his life with His matchless grace and love. On those three occasions, Christ called him by his original name, Simon, then gave him a new name, revealed to him Christ's true identity, and promised to pray for him for strength against spiritual failure.[8]

And now, here again in John 21:15-17, Christ uses that original name, Simon. It is no doubt calculated to call Peter's attention to those three special moments in the past. Jesus seems to be saying to Peter:

> "I'm using your original name to remind you that it was I Who called you by name from your small, humble village and occupation. It was My grace that opened your eyes to My real

identity. And though you've had many faults in life, My patience and grace have borne long with you, praying for you always. Therefore, right now, even though you feel like a spiritual failure, the same grace that did all this for you in the past will meet you again in what I'm about to do. Yes, you betrayed Me and rejected Me even with a curse. But My grace is here to meet you. I still love you, and in the light of My love for you, I'm once again calling you by your original name and asking whether you love Me."

Another observation we need to make concerning the John 21:15-17 passage focuses on the threefold repetition in Christ's dialogue with Peter:

1. Christ's threefold repetition of His questions to Peter ("Simon...do you love Me?").
2. Peter's threefold repetition of his answers to Christ ("Yes, Lord, You know I love You").
3. Christ's threefold repetition of commands to Peter ("Feed/take care of My lambs/sheep").

In the original language in which the New Testament was written, there is a very subtle stylistic variation, yet no vain repetition, in the threefold repetitions in our Lord's dialogue with Peter.[9] For the purpose of our discussion in this study, we will only consider the implications of the variations in the use of the word *love* during the dialogue.

Dialogue on Love

Here's how Christ's love conversation with Peter appears:

1. First Dialogue (v. 15)

    Jesus: "Simon, son of John, do you (*agape*) love Me more than these?"

    Peter: "Yes, Lord; You know that I (*philos*) love You."

2. Second Dialogue (v. 16)

Jesus: "Simon, son of John, do you (*agape*) love Me?"

Peter: "Yes, Lord; You know I (*philos*) love You."

3. Third Dialogue (v. 17)

Jesus: "Simon, son of John, do you (*philos*) love Me?"

Peter: "Lord, You know everything; You know that I (*philos*) love You."

In chapter 9 of this book ("Faces of Love"), we discussed the three major words for "love" that were used during New Testament times: *eros, philos,* and *agape*—the last two of which appear in the New Testament. The passage currently under consideration in John 21 employs these two words.

Notice that whereas in His first two questions Christ employed the verbal form of the word *agape* (principled, sacrificial love), in each of his replies to the Lord, Peter consistently used the verbal form of the word *philos* (affectionate, friendship love) for his love for Christ. But, in the third dialogue, Christ changed the verb He used in the two previous dialogues to the *philos* verb that Peter had consistently employed.

That is, in His last question to Peter, Christ changed from the verbal form of the word *agape* (selfless and sacrificial love) to that of *philos* (affectionate and friendship love). Christ was in effect asking him: "Simon, do you truly love Me as a friend? Are you really fond of Me? Do you have a deep affection for Me? Do you love (*philos*) Me as you claim, Peter?"

Some have suggested that supposedly, the Lord is asking Peter whether he has the higher form of love for Him—*agape*—but that Peter, his self-confidence shattered by his threefold betrayal of Jesus the night of His arrest, can only affirm a lower, weaker form of love (*philos*). Finally, the Lord descends to that lower level Himself in His third question.

I don't believe that the above explanation is either biblically or logically correct.

First, the Gospel writer John usually used the two verbs as synonyms, and often interchangeably.[10]

Second, if Jesus was supposedly descending to Peter's level, Peter's answer to the Lord's question the first two times should have been "No." That is, the Lord asked him if he had *agape* love for Him, and Peter should have said "No," meaning that now, in light of all that happened, he could only promise the supposed lower form of *philos* love. But that isn't what Peter says. He says in each case, "Lord, You know I (*philos*) love You." And he was hurt when the Lord asked the question the third time, as if He hadn't believed Peter the first two times.

These two facts suggest that we should not make a big deal out of the fact that the Gospel writer John used a different Greek verb in the third question. But while Jesus was not descending from His supposed higher level of *agape* to Peter's lower level of *philos,* I believe that there are at least two compelling reasons for Christ's variation for the word *love.* In other words, besides stylistic variations, there are at least two deeper reasons for Christ's use of the verbal form of *philos* in His last question.

First, the significance of the conversation doesn't lie in the different uses of the Greek words for love, but rather in the threefold utterance of the question, "Do you love Me?" By asking Peter this question three times, Jesus is alluding to Peter's three denials and seems to be giving the apostle an opportunity to take back his denial with a threefold assertion of his love and loyalty. Christ was, in effect, officially restoring Peter to his previous position of trust, especially since, in the eyes of the other disciples, Peter might have lost their trust for performing that awful deed of betrayal.

Second, and more important, it appears that John the Gospel writer may have used the word *philos* instead of *agape* to underscore the fact that there cannot be true affectionate, brotherly, *philos* love unless it is grounded in *agape* love. The change in the verbal form of the word was designed to point to the depth of love—the ground of true love.

Stated differently, Christ was asking Peter on whose terms he loved Him. What was the nature and foundation of Peter's *philos* love? Christ seems to be encouraging the apostle to ground his *philos* love in God's *agape* love through a more intimate knowledge of Christ.

The Ground of Love

Peter had always had a deep affection—*philos* love—for Jesus. Otherwise, why would he leave his job, friends, family, and all other preoccupations to follow Christ? He himself at one time had probed Jesus: "We have left everything to follow You! What then will there be for us?" (Matthew 19:27).

But notice this important point: Even though Peter's love was real, it shared in the law of cause and effect. As explained in chapter 9 of this book, unlike the selfless, sacrificial love of *agape,* the *philos* love of Peter, though real, expected something in return ("What then will there be for us?"). Peter's *philos* love, like *eros* love, had not yet matured into the principled love of *agape.* True love expects nothing in return, and only those who fully know God can have this kind of love.

As we pointed out earlier, Peter had three times denied being a follower of Jesus, claiming at least once: *"I don't know the Man."*[11] What Peter may not have realized at the time he spoke those words was that he was echoing a profound truth about himself: *Before his encounter with Jesus Christ, Peter had not really known Jesus at all. For to know Him is to love Him. And to love Him is to serve Him, no matter the cost.*

Because Peter didn't know Jesus, his *philos* love, however real it might have been, was not grounded in the divine principle of *agape* love—self-sacrificing love. For only those who know God can truly love God and others. The apostle John declares that "everyone who loves has been born of God and knows God. Whoever does not love does not know God, because God is love. . . . If we love one another, God lives in us and His love is made complete in us" (1 John 4:7, 8, 12).

In other words, without knowing God, there can be no *agape* love. And without *agape* love, *philos* love and *eros* love have no roots. True love is possible only when there is repentance and conversion—a total surrender to the Lord.

Stated differently, and at the risk of overly repeating myself, without *agape* love, *philos* love and *eros* love have no root. Without an intimate, experiential knowledge of God, we cannot love Him as we ought, and we cannot go all the way for Him, even to the point of death.

In a real sense, then, during the third time Christ used Peter's expression of (*philos*) love in His own question to the apostle (instead of the *agape* love employed in the first two questions), Christ was in effect pointing out to Peter that for any kind of love (whether *philos* or *eros*) to be real, it must be rooted in *agape* love—something possible if and only if a person knows God. Christ's question ("Do you love Me?") was therefore an invitation for Peter to "know" Him.

Until a person is broken, or totally surrendered to the Lord Jesus Christ, his or her love for Him or for any fellow human being is incomplete. It will be conditional, sharing in the law of cause and effect ("If you do this for me, then I will love you."). True love, however, is rooted in the divine, principled love called *agape*.

Human love tends to be only on the level of *philos* or *eros*. God's love is *agape*. Only when we have God in our lives—only when we know Him (not just know *about* Him)—can we truly love Him as well as our fellow human beings.

Experiencing True Love

As sinners, we are by nature self-centered. We operate by the principle of selfishness. We are motivated or driven primarily by our own self-interest. Everything we do and think about is prompted by self-seeking and self-gratification. Our whole preoccupation in life is for self. Our priorities and activities are designed to fulfill selfish interests.

Even the highest expression of love we know of, whether to God or to man, is self-love. When Jesus said, "Love your neighbor as yourself," the assumption in that statement is that man naturally loves self![12] In contrast to Christ's "self-emptying" act that resulted in His giving His life for us, our self-love or self-centeredness partakes of Lucifer's selfishness and leads to destruction.[13]

Selfishness is the root cause of our natural obsession with getting but not giving. This self-centeredness is the reason why, like Peter, even when we "forsake all" in order to follow Jesus, we do so because of "what will be there for us." True love begins when we acknowledge that we have a problem with selfishness and we need help. Three steps are involved.

To experience love we must first have God in our lives. To do so *we must first acknowledge (with Peter) that we have failed God—we have betrayed Him in our lives.* Consequently, even our profession of love is selfish. We love God and our fellow human beings for what we can get from them. Words, such as the following, betray the lack of depth of our love:

"I love you because . . .

- you make me laugh."
- you're a wonderful person."
- we get along so well."
- you have strong faith."
- you are so beautiful."
- of how I feel when I'm with you."
- you care about meeting my needs."
- you bring me pleasure and make me happy."

Second, *we must recognize that of ourselves, we cannot love God or even any other person.* We simply cannot do it in our own power. Peter thought he would never betray the trust of Christ. He was self-confident. He trusted himself. He didn't know that he had no power in himself to carry out his own choice. Because he relied on his own power, he failed miserably.

How many times have *we* also made commitments to love another person—even "for better or for worse, for richer or poorer"—only to betray or fail that person when things actually got better, worse, richer, or poorer? We can only succeed in honoring our love commitments if we totally surrender our lives to God.[14]

Third, *we must ask God to search our hearts, forgive us our sins, and give us the power to love Him and others.* Peter did all this, when in his contrition he deferred to the God "Who knows all things," including our weaknesses and failures. When this God becomes the Lord of our lives, He will impart to us His *agape* love and purify the other types of human love we already have.

God has made provision for this special gift through the death of our Lord Jesus Christ on our behalf. "For God so loved the world that He gave His one and only Son, that whoever believes in Him shall not perish but have eternal life" (John 3:16).

The Evidence of Love

Though love is an invisible entity, its fruits are clearly seen. As stated in the opening chapter of this book,

Where There's Love . . .

It is always known
It can't be kept to its own
Because you're on its heart's throne

True love is visible in what it does. Thus, the answer to the question, "Do you love Me?" is seen in what you do for Jesus. That is why Jesus said in another place, "If you love Me, keep My commandments."[15] In other words, if we love Jesus, we must do something with that love.

Contrary to the assertions of counterfeit love, true love is not simply a feeling or an emotion of the heart. It is primarily an *action.* If you love Jesus, it will be seen practically. You will inevitably demonstrate your love for Jesus—or your lack of love for Him—by what you do in the time you are granted by God to live and move.

Three important demands were placed upon Peter as evidence of his restored love.

First, our Lord made it clear that if Peter truly loved Him, he would feed and take care of Christ's lambs and sheep.[16] In other words, *true love serves the object of its affection.*

In our self-serving love culture, love is defined by how a person serves you in the relationship. But in the love rooted in the *agape* love of Christ, true love is measured by how you serve others. You serve by giving selflessly, even if doing so hurts or even kills you.

Second, *true love is costly.* After urging Peter to feed or care for His flock, our Lord made this intriguing statement to the apostle:

> "I tell you the truth, when you were younger you dressed yourself and went where you wanted; but when you are old you will stretch out your hands and someone else will dress you and lead you where you do not want to go." Jesus said this to indicate the kind of death by which Peter would glorify God. Then He said to him, "Follow Me!" (John 21:18, 19).

In effect, our Lord was saying that true love, the love that serves others, is also a love that is costly. Instead of getting something in return, it would rather give everything, including life itself, for Christ! The introductory statement, "I tell you the truth" (or as the King James Version of the Bible renders it, "Verily, verily, I say unto thee"), asserts that the costly nature of love is not a probability or possibility but a certainty.

Finally, *true love will go all the way with and for Jesus.* Having mentioned that his love for the Lord will cost Peter his life, Jesus told the apostle, "Follow Me" (John 21:19, 22). This was the same invitation He had given Peter three years earlier. At that time Peter "left everything to follow" the Lord. But he did so with the expectation of "what will be there for us?"

But now that his *philos* love has been transformed by his conversion and grounded in the *agape* love of God, through an intimate knowledge of Christ, the apostle is invited again to "follow" the Lord. True love always follows Christ wherever He leads, even if it doesn't know where the path will lead. As long as the "following" will glorify God, true love will go all the way the Saviour leads. In the words of David Livingstone,

"Lord, send me anywhere, only go with me.
Lay any burden on me, only sustain me.

Sever any ties but the tie that binds me to Thy service and to Thy heart."

Response to Love

In the preceding two chapters we discovered that our irresistible desire to be loved is matched by the far greater passion of God's love for us. *We* need love, and *He* has committed Himself to love us. In the words of the prophet Jeremiah, "The Lord has appeared of old unto me, saying, Yea, I have loved thee with an everlasting love: therefore with lovingkindness have I drawn thee" (Jeremiah 31:3).

But despite His love, something went terribly wrong. We let Him down. We hurt Him by turning our backs on Him, betraying Him, denying Him, and nailing Him to the cross. But now, despite all that we have done to our resurrected Lord Jesus Christ, He is asking us: "Do you love Me?"

The simplest, yet most profound question you can ever be asked to answer is: "Do you love Jesus?"

If your answer is "Yes," then take that love and turn it into action by serving Him and others, however costly it may be.

But if you cannot say "Yes" to Jesus, I want to ask you, "Why not?" Is there anyone or anything else worth loving more than Jesus?

Only when we respond affirmatively and prove our love for Him by our actions can we ever expect to experience the real beauty and joy of His matchless love. To this we shall now turn our attention.

Notes:

1. Matthew 26:33, 35.
2. Matthew 19:27; cf. Luke 5:11.
3. Matthew 16:16.
4. Observe that Peter had three times denied being a follower of Jesus, claiming at least one time that "I don't know the Man" (Matthew 26:69-75; cf. Mark 14:66-72; Luke 22:55-62; John 18:15-27).
5. Matthew 26:32; cf. Mark 14:28.

6. Mark 16:7; Matthew 28:7; cf. v. 10.

7. For example, Galilee was the place where Peter walked on the water with Jesus. It was in that vicinity that he saw Jesus cast out demons, heal the bleeding woman, raise Jairus's daughter to life, and feed five thousand. In John 21:4-6, Jesus provides a miraculous catch of fish, when previously they could catch none—similar to the events described when Christ first called Peter in Luke 5. Also, in John 21:7 Peter jumps into the sea to greet Jesus when he discovers who He is, just as when Peter walked on the sea, in Matthew 14. Furthermore, in John 21:9-14, there is a meal together, made on burning coals, with fish and bread. The fish and bread pointed back to the feeding of the five thousand, the smoldering coal fire pointed back to the coal fire at Peter's denial in the palace, and the meal together may have recalled the last supper they had had together.

8. Prior to this post-resurrection encounter in Galilee, there were three occasions in the past when Jesus called Peter by his original name, Simon: namely, John 1:42; Matthew 16:16, 17; and Luke 22:31, 32. Notice the previous contexts of the use of Peter's original name: (1) John 1:42 was to remind Peter of his humble extraction, when he first met the Lord and was given another name, Cephas (a stone). It was an act of grace when Peter first met the Lord. Grace found him at that time. (2) Matthew 16:16, 17 recounted when, in response to Jesus' question about His true identity, Peter answered: "You are Christ, the Son of the living God." Following this confession of faith, our Lord then said to Peter that it was not flesh and blood that revealed the deity of the Son of God to him. It was an act of grace, when Heaven chose to reveal this insightful revelation to Peter. (3) Luke 22:31, 32 records how, shortly before Christ's crucifixion, our Lord had said to Peter: "Simon, Simon, Satan has asked to sift you as wheat. But I have prayed for you, Simon, that your faith may not fail. And when you have turned back, strengthen your brothers."

9. The passage contains a remarkable variety of synonyms in the Greek: (a) Two different Greek words for "love" are used (*agape* and *philos*); (b) two different Greek words for "feed" are used (*boske* and *poimane*); (c) two different Greek words for the "flock" to be cared for are used (*arnion* and *probata*); and (d) two different Greek words for "know" are used (*oida* and *ginosko*).

10. For example, John refers to himself in the Gospel as "the disciple whom Jesus loved" and uses both verbs in that description. Both verbs are used in this Gospel in statements about the love the Father has for the Son, both verbs are used of Jesus' love for Lazarus, and both verbs are used of the Father's love for His people. Compare how it is used for the love of the Father for the Son in John 3:35 (*agape*) and 5:20 (*philos*); the Father's love for the believer in 14:21 (*agape*) and 16:27 (*philos*); and the Son's love for a

certain disciple in 13:23 (*agape*) and 20:2 (*philos*).

11. Matthew 26:69-75; cf. Mark 14:66-72; Luke 22:55-62; John 18:15-27.

12. Matthew 19:19; cf. Ephesians 5:28, 29.

13. Philippians 2:5-8; cf. Isaiah 14:12-16.

14. Describing how we can overcome our inherent inability to love God or any other person, one Christian devotional writer explains the process of totally surrendering ourselves to God: "Many are inquiring, '*How* am I to make the surrender of myself to God?' You desire to give yourself to Him, but you are weak in moral power, in slavery to doubt, and controlled by the habits of your life of sin. Your promises and resolutions are like ropes of sand. You cannot control your thoughts, your impulses, your affections. The knowledge of your broken promises and forfeited pledges weakens your confidence in your own sincerity, and causes you to feel that God cannot accept you; but you need not despair. What you need to understand is the true force of the will. This is the governing power in the nature of man, the power of decision, or of choice. Everything depends on the right action of the will. The power of choice God has given to men; it is theirs to exercise. You cannot change your heart, you cannot of yourself give to God its affections; but you can choose to serve Him. You can give Him your will; He will then work in you to will and to do according to His good pleasure. Thus your whole nature will be brought under the control of the Spirit of Christ; your affections will be centered upon Him, your thoughts will be in harmony with Him." See Ellen G. White, *Steps to Christ* (Mountain View, Calif.: Pacific Press, 1956), p. 47.

15. John 14:15.

16. John 21:15-17.

PART VI

CONCLUSION

20

THE BEAUTY OF LOVE

"One word frees us of all the weight and pain in life.
That word is Love."
~Socrates~

True love finds it difficult to explain in human words why it loves and how to honor its object of affection. That is why poetry is often the *lingua franca* for those living in the world of intimate love relationships, whether human or divine. Let me illustrate what I mean.

Just as I was completing this book manuscript, a friend shared with me some original poems that a man had written to her at different times in their courtship. Three of the love poems immediately caught my attention. The first (the title of which is derived from the acronym of my friend's name), explains the man's difficulty in describing why he dearly loved her. The second builds upon the first and imagines the day when their relationship would be sealed at the marriage altar. The third poem looks beyond the wedding day to a life that would be "inseparable for eternity."

Cherish Her Always Until Numberless Days Restored Appear
In the darkest hour of Earth's history I have light.

Your smile is to me as the rising sun,
Your happiness as the clear blue sky,
And your voice as the graceful flight of colorful birds.
You fill my thoughts with loveliness and give vision to my speech.
Yet, and still, these illustrations are as the fin-
ger paintings of a child—
Beautiful in their effort, but far deficient in cap-
turing the portrait of my love for you.

My Priceless Treasure

I long to appreciate you more, but I am bankrupt of the resources.
How can an unworthy man impress a daughter of the King?
I excavate my heart for treasures that I may present to you.
And though golden words like precious jewels are uncovered,
They fail to satisfy my hunger to honor you.
I desire for the world to know you are a priceless gift—
A gift not procured by my own merits.
Your companionship to me is the embodiment of grace.
I dare not say I deserved you or to be received by you.
I simply respond to the irresistible force of your welcome.
Your open arms are stronger than the pull of gravity,
Lifting me above all sorrow to embrace joy.
As I journey beyond the earthly experi-
ence, my senses are made alive.
And I can now see eternity in our commitment,
Grabbing hold of victory when I touch your hand,
And have a foretaste of HEAVEN with you as my wife.
My thoughts are fragrant with the aroma of you,
And the combination of our names, like the harmony of a choir.
You are my assurance in the hope of reality,
More fantastic than the imagination can conjure.

The Lady Who Will Be My W.I.F.E.

If the unveiling of my heart pleases you,
Witness the revelation of my love.
Exposing feelings that remained sealed from the view of most,
I have singled you out.
You do I claim as my own,

Placing you upon a pedestal as the trophy I've won.
United together we rise above the massive population,
As the symbol of true love.
Not subject to space or time;
No distance between us can affect your proximity to my heart.
Though the sands of the hourglass beat down upon it continually,
It shall not erode.
The substance of this love is divine in origin,
Established for the purpose of endurance.
Our foundation is in Eden and our pinnacle in the City of God.
Faith is the structure of our success,
And the promises of God our blueprints.
With Christ as the Master Builder and Architect,
I shall stand as your man with you beside me as—
My **W**oman **I**nseparable **F**or **E**ternity.

The Intimacy of Love

Indeed, those who have ever been in love will readily acknowledge that true love always "desires for the world to know" that its object of affection is the world's most "priceless gift." But as the above poems aptly illustrate, even after excavating the heart and uncovering golden words like "precious jewels," these terms cannot adequately capture the deepest longings of love to explain why it loves and how to honor its object of affection.

The same difficulty is captured in the Bible. On the one hand, Heaven wants to tell how much God loves us. Yet human words are inadequate to express it. That is why God sent His Son into the world to reveal what true love is.

Prior to Christ's coming into the world, the Bible conjured many imageries—from intimate human relationships and even nature—to explain God's love for humanity. Nowhere is God's love better revealed than in the Old Testament book of Song of Songs. This book is the greatest and the most moving love poem ever written by man. It portrays the love that Christ was later to reveal to the world.

Because the Bible is about love—God's love for humanity—something would have been lacking in the Holy Scriptures if they had not contained any expression for the deepest and strongest sentiment of humanity. The Song of Songs is the one book in the Bible that celebrates this beauty and intimacy of love—love between an exalted, royal bridegroom and his bride of humble extraction.

The bridegroom is a king called Solomon, or *Shelomoh*—the richest king ever to rule Israel. The bride is a poor country girl. Strangely, her real name is never given. She is simply called "the Shulamite," or *Shûlammîth*—the feminine form of *Shelomoh*. If this love poem had been written today, we would say that it is describing the relationship between Mr. and Mrs. Solomon.

As we reflect upon the inspired love poems in the Song of Songs, we will discover (a) the unfolding of the infinite and unchanging love of an exalted Bridegroom, (b) the development and growth of the love of His humble bride, and (c) how she is brought into the enjoyment of His love and raised from her lowly position to share the throne of her exalted Groom. The Bridegroom is none other than Christ, and the bride is God's people, corporately and individually—all those who, throughout the ages of time, have faithfully loved the Lord.[1]

The Greatest Story of Love

The account of the love relationship in the Song of Songs reads like a lover's diary. It does not seem to follow a chronological sequence but comes in bits and pieces. When the book begins, the Shulamite is in King Solomon's palace. But as one reads the book, it becomes evident that she has not always been there. She and her family had apparently been taking care of one of the king's vineyards in the countryside. This vineyard was close to Baal-hamon, in the northernmost part of Galilee, near the foothills of the mountains of Lebanon (8:11).

The love story began one day when the king, taking a few days off from his busy royal affairs, went to visit his vineyard in the country. And there he saw the Shulamite woman and fell in love with her. Disguising himself as a shepherd, he spent time with her, favored her with his kindness, and eventually won her heart. He then later revealed his true identity to her and brought her back to the palace with him (1:6-8).

Though the country girl initially felt out of place in the palace, she later felt at home and developed a passionate love for the king. But as the love story unfolds, it appears that at one point in their relationship, she took him for granted, and due to her own lethargy and hesitancy to respond to a different manifestation of the king's love, there was a separation in the relationship. The king left (see 5:2-6).

In desperation, the Shulamite rises and seeks him in the night, though she "could not find him." She called, but he gave her "no answer" (5:6). Sad and anxious, she endures bitter disappointment as she is oppressed by the heartless insult and injury of those who are indifferent to her woes. But she does not give up. Wounded, weary, and lovesick, she turns to the daughters of Jerusalem for their assistance. She urges them: "I charge you, O daughters of Jerusalem, If you find my beloved, that you tell him I am lovesick!" (5:8).

The daughters of Jerusalem cannot understand why this beautiful woman (described as "fairest among women"[2]) would be so desperate in searching for her beloved. They ask her: What is so unique about your lover? Can't you find any another man to love? To quote their twice-uttered question: "How is your beloved better than others, most beautiful of women? How is your beloved better than others, that you charge us so?" (5:9).

Without a moment's hesitation, the Shulamite offers a passionate description of her beloved. She describes him from head to toe, giving an account of his appearance, features, and glory. The excellencies and attractiveness of the groom are set forth in verses 10-16:

My beloved is white and ruddy,
The chiefest among ten thousand.

His head is as the most fine gold,
His locks are bushy, and black as a raven.
His eyes are as the eyes of doves
By the rivers of waters,

Washed with milk, and fitly set.
His cheeks are as a bed of spices,
As sweet flowers:
His lips like lilies,
Dropping sweet smelling myrrh.

His hands are as gold rings
Set with the beryl:
His belly is as bright ivory
Overlaid with sapphires.

His legs are as pillars of marble,
Set upon sockets of fine gold:
His countenance is as Lebanon,
Excellent as the cedars.

His mouth is most sweet:
Yea, he is altogether lovely.
This is my beloved,
And this is my friend,
O daughters of Jerusalem.

Worthy of note is that there are ten specific descriptions of the groom's features—the head, hair, eyes, cheeks, lips, hands, belly, legs, countenance, and mouth. These are sandwiched between the Shulamite's overall estimation of her king-lover at the beginning and at the end of the passage under consideration.

She begins, "My beloved is white and ruddy, the chiefest of ten thousand" (v. 10), and she concludes by stating of him, "Yea, he is altogether lovely. This is my beloved, and this is my friend" (v. 16). The introduction asserts the preeminence or superiority of the groom above all others. And the conclusion reiterates why this man, who is altogether lovely, is her special object of affection.

The passionate description that the Shulamite bride gives of her kingly bridegroom finds its fulfillment only in our glorious risen Lord, Jesus Christ. It is His perfections that pass before us. As we reflect upon the bride's detailed description of Solomon, the royal groom sitting upon the throne of David, we shall discover that it also fittingly describes our Lord Jesus Christ, the royal Bridegroom Who is the true Son of David. Significantly, this inspired poem also reveals what true love is all about.[3]

THE EXCELLENCE OF LOVE

Before going into specific details of the groom's outward appearance, the bride asserts the preeminence of the groom's inward beauty above that of all others. Let's now look at how the excellence of Christ's love is captured in the passage.

It is Christ's preeminence that is first emphasized, when He is described as "the Chiefest among ten thousand" (v. 10). But we must note that the reason He excels all others in every respect—whether teachers, leaders, philosophers, or saviors of society—is because He is "white and ruddy." This expression aptly describes His matchless purity and sacrificial spirit.

The "white" refers to His spotless purity or sinlessness, and the "ruddy" (or red) points to the stain of His precious, sacrificial blood. His holiness is such as the world has never seen. And His atoning death is that which draws all men unto Himself.

This is the reason why the red stains of our sins can be forgiven, and we can be pure in His holy sight. Christ's sinless life and atoning death are the basis of God's promise to us: "Though your sins are like scarlet, they shall be as white as snow; though they are red like crimson, they shall be as wool" (Isaiah 1:18).

Among all human beings Christ stands alone, for He is sinless. And among all philanthropists—people who are known for their general love for, or benevolence toward, the whole of humankind—Christ takes the highest place, for "He gave Himself for us." Calvary is the proof of His matchless love.[4]

No wonder He is depicted as "white and ruddy, the Chiefest among ten thousand." Whatever others may be, Christ is "the Chiefest." However many there may be, Christ is "the Chiefest among ten thousand." His incomparable purity and sacrificial spirit sets Jesus apart from all others. The following ten descriptions explain in greater detail why He is preeminent over all others.

1. His Majesty. The king's supreme stateliness or impressive splendor is indicated by the description, "His head is as the most fine gold" (5:11).[5] The words *most fine gold* indicate the "gold of gold"—choice gold, or gold that has been refined to the uttermost. This could be an indication of Christ's virtue, value, and glory. As fine gold is known for its shining brightness, so Christ is "the brightness of His (the Father's) glory, and the express image of His person."[6]

As the "Head," Christ stands above all others as the most outstanding Leader. The same holds true in the church. His headship is unparalleled, for the New Testament says concerning Him: "He is the Head of the body, the church, Who is the Beginning, the Firstborn from the dead, that in all things He may have the preeminence."[7] He is head-above-shoulders in every respect—within and without the church.

2. His Strength. After calling attention to his head, the logical feature the Shulamite mentions is the hair on her groom's head. "His locks are bushy, and black as a raven" (5:11). His locks are flowing and black, suggesting the vigor of manhood.

This also points to our Lord Jesus Christ. Though He was fully divine, He was also fully human. Yet, He was man at his best, full of life and health.

Of Ephraim it is said, "Strangers have devoured his strength, and he knoweth it not: yea, grey hairs are here and there upon him, yet he knoweth not."[8] But of Ephraim's Lord—our Lord and King—no signs of decay shall ever be seen. His "bushy" locks suggest "no white hair, no trace of age or decay will ever pass on Him. Where all grows old, He never grows old. His years shall never fail."[9]

Our Lord "Jesus never changes. His character never varies! His power never diminishes! His glory never fades! His truth never deviates! His promises never fail! Bless His name, His is 'the same yesterday, and today, and forever' (Hebrews 13:8)."[10] And because He never changes, He is dependable!

3. His Tenderness. Continuing the description of the groom, the bride adds, "His eyes are as the eyes of doves by the rivers of waters, washed with milk, and fitly set." She likens the groom's eyes to a dove's eyes, and the dove is well known for its tender compassion, gentle nature, and winsomeness. The "rivers of waters," the restful environment frequented by doves, could also refer to the restfulness of his gaze.

What better description of our Lord Jesus Christ, Whose tender eyes are so pure that they appear as "washed with milk." With His all-seeing, caring eyes, He knows and understands all that is going on in the lives of His children, "for the eyes of the Lord run to and fro throughout the whole earth, to show Himself strong in the behalf of them whose heart is perfect toward Him."[11]

Centuries later, the prophet Habakkuk wrote concerning our God: "Your eyes are too pure to look on evil; You cannot tolerate wrong."[12] Such are the keen eyes of our Lord. But the believer does not have to fear His penetrating glance. For there is grace and mercy in His look—the kind of look that melted Peter's heart after he thrice betrayed his Lord.

The expression, His "fitly set" eyes, implies that they neither protrude nor sink in. They are like the precious stone that is perfectly set in the thin metal foil of the ring. They are charming and pleasant to behold. Christ promises us: "I will guide you with My eyes" (Psalm 32:8)—His winsome, affectionate eyes.

It has also been observed that a male dove will not look upon any other dove but his mate. In the same vein, Christ's eyes are passionately and endearingly fixed on His children. His eyes are not only full of tenderness but also full of faithfulness!

Since our Lord's tender eyes are always upon us, the Bible invites us also to "fix our eyes upon Jesus" (Hebrews 12:2). For when we turn our eyes upon Him and look full in His wonderful face, the things of Earth will grow strangely dim in the light of His glory and grace.

4. His Attractiveness. Another aspect of the royal groom's features, highlighted by the Shulamite, are his cheeks. "His cheeks are as a bed of spices, as sweet flowers" (v. 13a). The appearance of the cheeks often reveals the beauty, attractiveness, and health of a person's face.

As is true of other descriptions, this feature of the groom also points to our Lord Jesus Christ. "The world saw no beauty in Christ, and smote Him on the cheek. Judas professed attraction to Christ but only to betray Him by kissing Him on the cheek. The believer, on the other hand, can delight in the beauty and attractiveness of Christ as a bed of fragrant herbs calls forth the admiration of the passerby."[13]

When the cheeks are depicted "as a bed of spices" and "as sweet flowers" or "towers of perfumes" (as the marginal reference appropriately renders it), these expressions are emphasizing the perfect sweetness and fragrant beauty of Christ's face. To behold Him is to fall in love with Him!

5. His Words. Before moving on to another part of the king's physical anatomy, his admirer comments about his lips. "His lips [are] like lilies, dropping sweet smelling myrrh" (v. 13b). This comparison suggests the purity and the sweet-smelling myrrh of his gracious words.

This description also points to the words of Christ, which are pure words, free from all foulness, deceit, and flattery. His words are pleasant, gracious, and graceful. Contrast Christ's speech with what the Bible says concerning words from unrenewed human lips: "Their talk is foul, like the stench from an open grave. Their tongues are filled with lies. Snake venom drips from their lips. Their mouths are full of cursing and bitterness."[14]

Even the prophet Isaiah had to confess that he was a man of unclean lips.[15] But the lips of Christ were pure; no guile was found in His mouth. And of Christ it can also be said, "Grace is poured into Thy lips" (Psalm 45:2). "Never man spake like this Man," was the testimony of officers who were sent by the leading priests and Pharisees to arrest Jesus.[16]

As our Lord passed through this world, words of grace, pardon, righteousness, salvation, and life were ever dropping from His lips like sweet-smelling myrrh. He spoke, and the winds and waves obeyed Him. The lips of Jesus, and His only, can speak peace to our troubled souls.

In the words of the now-familiar nineteenth-century devotional writer and author of *The Desire of Ages*, Christ "did not suppress one word of truth, but He spoke it always in love. He exercised the greatest tact, and thoughtful, kind attention in His intercourse with the people. He was never rude, never needlessly spoke a severe word, never gave needless pain to a sensitive soul. He did not censure human weakness. He fearlessly denounced hypocrisy, unbelief, and iniquity, but tears were in His voice as He uttered His scathing rebukes."[17]

Christ's words were always appropriate and enjoyable. He knew how to "speak a word in season to him that is weary."[18] The words were not dropped scantily but poured out carefully. One Bible commentator describes the manner in which the delivery of Christ's words is said to be like a "dropping:" (1) Gradually—not all at once, but little by little so that we can bear them; (2) Seasonably, at proper times, as the wants of people require; (3) Constantly, He speaks through various agencies and through His ministers in all ages to win His children into the kingdom; (4) Sweetly and gently, not like sudden torrents of rain.[19]

Our Lord spoke profound truths in language so simple that His audience could not fail of understanding. "His instruction was so direct, His illustrations were so appropriate, His words so sympathetic and cheerful, that His hearers were charmed."[20] The simplicity and earnestness with which He addressed His audiences, hallowed His tender, gracious words.

6. His Works. The exceptionally formed limbs of the groom are next described: "His hands are as gold rings set with the beryl" (v. 14a). This is an apparent reference to the value and the enduring nature of the works of his hands.

In considering the hands of our Lord Jesus Christ, we cannot help but think of all His works or accomplishments—what He has done, what He is doing, and what He will do. These include His works of nature, providence, and grace. Like gold, these works of the Lord are of great value and are as enduring and substantial as His matchless character. We are told in Scripture that "the works of His hands are verity and judgment; all His commandments are sure. They stand fast forever and ever, and are done in truth and uprightness."[21]

But of all His works, Christ's work of redemption on Calvary stands out most boldly. Human beings expressed their hatred of our Lord by nailing His hands of love to a cross. But the believer delights in His hands, for those very hands remind us that He will never forget us or cease to have compassion upon us. He Himself spoke through the prophet Isaiah when He said, "Behold, I have graven thee upon the palms of My hands" (Isaiah 49:15, 16). And the palms of His hands bear the marks of the wounds that He received at Calvary.

But even more, through the eternal ages to come, the marks in His precious hands will show forth His praise and declare His power to save and to sustain His children. Those memorial wounds on His hands will ever remind us of His love. Looking forward to that day in the far future, the Old Testament prophet Zechariah foretold this about Christ: "One shall say unto Him, 'What are these wounds in Thine hands?' Then He shall answer, 'Those with which I was wounded in the house of My friends'" (Zechariah 13:6).

Thus, "His hands [that] are as gold rings set with the beryl" point to the value and the enduring nature of His redemptive work. Today, all power is in those hands of Christ to uphold and sustain His children. In the words of a familiar chorus, "He's got the whole world in His hands."

We should, however, never forget that the hand that wields the power is a hand that is moved by love. It is a hand that offers a warm embrace. Elsewhere in the Song of Songs, this intimate embrace is thus described: "His left hand is under my head, and his right hand doth embrace me" (2:6). Our Lord will lovingly embrace any repentant soul. And in the words of a poem in chapter 3 of this book, He will say to that soul:

"My embrace will always warm your heart,
And only death will force us apart."

7. His Compassion. Up until this time, the Shulamite had been describing only the visible features of her love. But now she turns to a hidden detail of her groom's body: "His belly is as bright ivory overlaid with sapphires" (v. 14b).

In Scriptures, the belly has to do with the deep inner emotions. Sometimes, the same word is rendered in characteristic Hebrew terms as "bowels."[22] The reference to "bright ivory overlaid with sapphires" could be a reference to the purity or heavenly origin of his feelings and the glory of his tender compassion.

The inner feelings and sensitivity of Christ's deep emotions are being highlighted here. Pure as the "bright ivory" and deep as the bowels is the tenderness, pity, compassion, and love of our Lord Jesus Christ. Scriptures tell us that "His compassions fail not. They are new every morning."[23] Borrowing the words of the apostle Paul, there is "consolation" in Christ; there is "comfort" in His love; there is "fellowship" in His Spirit; and there are "bowels and mercies" in His very being (Philippians 2:1).

As ivory was originally obtained from the tusk of a newly slain or dead elephant, so also Christ's sensitivity is rooted in His sufferings and death. One of the most beautiful sentiments recorded in the Bible is found in Isaiah, chapter 63, verse 9. It reads: "In all their affliction He was afflicted." It means that Christ sympathizes with His people in all their trials and that He is ever ready to aid them. He has "compassion on the ignorant, and on them that are out of the way; for that He Himself also is compassed with infirmity" (Hebrews 5:2).

"Christ alone had experience in all the sorrows and temptations that befall human beings. Never another of woman born was so fiercely beset by temptation; never another bore so heavy a burden of the world's sin and pain. Never was there another whose sympathies were so broad or so tender. A sharer in all the experiences of humanity, He could feel not only for, but with, every burdened and tempted and struggling one."[24]

Our Saviour bore all that we are called upon to bear, so that no human being could say, "He does not know my suffering and my trials." In the words of my favorite author,

"He Who took humanity upon Himself knows how to sympathize

with the sufferings of humanity. Not only does Christ know every soul, and the peculiar needs and trials of that soul, but He knows all the circumstances that chafe and perplex the spirit. His hand is outstretched in pitying tenderness to every suffering child. Those who suffer most have most of His sympathy and pity. He is touched with the feeling of our infirmities, and He desires us to lay our perplexities and troubles at His feet and leave them there."[25]

8. His Stability. Another interesting feature of the groom to arrest the attention of the bride is his legs. "His legs are as pillars of marble, set in sockets of fine gold" (v. 15a). Since the legs bear up or carry the weight of the body, this description bespeaks his secure or stable foundation. Comparing legs to "pillars" or columns set in "sockets of fine gold" further emphasizes the proven strength and endurance of the lower part of his body.

This description also aptly fits the steadiness and steadfastness of our heavenly King. His legs are strong to support every weight we place upon Him. In the words of one Bible commentator, "The weighty purposes of God are founded upon Him! He bears up under the world, the heavens, the universe. Upon Him, the church is built, the saints are established. He is the immutable Christ, standing firm and unmovable forever."[26]

Because His legs are not shaky or wobbly, we can trust Christ with all our burdens of life. His strong legs can carry the loads of our trials and afflictions and the heaviness of our sorrows. No wonder Simon Peter said, "[Cast] all your care upon Him; for He careth for you" (1 Peter 5:7). He is, indeed, "able to keep us from falling, and to present us faultless before the presence of His glory with exceeding joy" (Jude 24).

9. His Countenance. Having described the unique features of her groom from head to foot, the bride now calls attention to his general appearance. She describes how all the specific features fit together in his full, overall stature or bearing. She declares, "His countenance is as Lebanon, excellent as the cedars" (v. 15b).

The countenance or "bearing" signifies the entire aspect of his being. This figure, evidently, illustrates the excellence and dignity of

Christ—His glorious majesty as the Messiah. His stature is likened to the lofty cedars of Lebanon—trees that exceeded others in height, endurance, and grandeur. His countenance is nobler, stronger, and greater than all others. This description highlights the unrivaled beauty and splendor of our Lord.

We also join the Shulamite bride in inviting you to take another look at our Lord Jesus Christ. You've seen the particular features of His character, His words, and His works. Now, stand back and look at His overall bearing. See if you can find anyone as noble, lovely, and majestic as our heavenly Groom.

If you take another look at our glorious Cedar of Lebanon, your heart will be inspired to shout Hallelujah! (Praise the Lord!) When you see how Christ combines in Himself commanding dignity with the winning grace of humility, when you behold how He unites in His person an unyielding firmness with gentleness, and when you catch a glimpse of how He managed to join His innocence and the simplicity of a child with His manly strength, you cannot but acknowledge how He merits the title King of kings and Lord of lords. And together with George Frideric Handel, the composer of the "Hallelujah Chorus," you also will sing "He shall reign forever and ever . . . King of kings, and Lord of lords . . . Hallelujah, Hallelujah!"

10. His Sweetness. The final feature in the bride's description of her groom is his mouth. She simply states, "His mouth is most sweet" (v. 16). The word *mouth* indicates more than "lips" that had previously been mentioned (v. 13). The Hebrew word is translated elsewhere as "taste." It has to do with the palate of the mouth. In the imagery of the Song of Songs, "the mouth" refers to the *kiss* of the mouth rather than the speech of the lips.

The bride's glowing description of the mouth as "most sweet," or more literally, "sweetnesses," points to the sweet tokens of Christ's love. His kisses are kisses of assurance and kindness. No wonder the first full verse that initiates this greatest love poem in the Bible, the Song of Songs, expresses the promptings of the bride to the groom: "Let him kiss me with the kisses of his mouth"! (1:2).

There are many kisses in the world, but only Christ's kiss can satisfy the heart. Once the Lord kisses us "with the kisses of His mouth," we shall discover that, indeed, the Lord is sweet. He is all "sweetnesses." Elsewhere in the Bible, King David may have been pointing to Jesus Christ, the Lord of David, when he wrote: "O taste and see that the Lord is good: blessed is the man that trusteth in Him" (Psalm 34:8).

All those who have tasted of Christ's grace can say from experience, "His mouth is most sweet." The grace and kindness with which He meets us, even after we repeatedly fail Him, is enough to impress the heart forever with the sweetness of the Lord's grace. Thus, the apostle Peter writes, "Ye have tasted that the Lord is gracious" (1 Peter 2:3).

The kisses of this world are like the kisses of Judas. They are kisses of betrayal and of death. But the kisses of our Lord Jesus Christ are kisses of grace, friendship, kindness, and love. Taste and see, and you also will know that "His mouth is most sweet"!

This Is Love!

Having said all she could say to describe the preeminence of the king's love, the Shulamite now concludes with the words, "Yea, he is altogether lovely. This is my beloved, and this is my friend, O daughters of Jerusalem" (v. 16). "Yea" is an old way of saying, "There is no doubt in my mind" or "Without question." She is "absolutely positive" that her groom is "altogether lovely."

What a fitting way to conclude! Everything about him, from top to bottom, "is altogether lovely." The literal translation is, "The whole of him is desires." He is everything she needs, and everything she desires. Can anyone doubt that this is a description of our Lord Jesus Christ?

The prophet Haggai calls Him "The Desire of all nations" (Haggai 2:7), and my favorite author calls Him "The Desire of ages." And we may also call Him "The Desire of all hearts," for He is the One all hearts yearn for. He has enough, and more than enough, to satisfy all our hearts' desires, to fill all the yearnings of the heart. In Christ we have One Who is altogether lovely. With Him, the heart can rest satisfied. He is all that we need!

Explaining why Jesus is "altogether lovely," one Bible commentator has said: "In His Person and character Christ is a Being Who commands and attracts the love of all who are susceptible to the charms of spiritual excellence. There is beauty beyond that which is physical. . . . Others have their excellences, but they have also their defects. In Him alone every virtue is present and complete, in Him alone every blemish is absent. He is at once above all praise and free from all blame."[27]

From whatever angle you look at Him, Christ is altogether lovely—from left to right, from top to bottom, from inside out. "The whole of Him is desires."

But there is one more thing to say about Him. When language fails to describe our Lord Jesus Christ—when adjectives, superlatives, and word pictures are inadequate to say all we need to say about our exalted King-Lover—let us conclude with the "fairest among women," the Shulamite bride, and say, "This is my Beloved, and this is my Friend."

He in Whom all these excellent qualities shine so brightly is actually . . . *my Beloved and my Friend!* It's simply amazing! In case you are wondering what kind of Friend He is, I will answer:

He is an *ever-present* Friend. He is always at hand when we call.
He is an *able* Friend. He has all the resources to help us.
He is a *willing* Friend. He's both able and ever
ready to assist us in times of our need.
He is a *faithful* Friend. He never fails or lets anyone down.
He is a *gracious* Friend. He understands
our failures and forgives our sins.
He is a *tenderhearted* Friend. He sympathizes with all
our trials, afflictions, disappointments, and sorrows.
He is an *unchangeable and unchanging* Friend. He never grows
cold or old, for He is the same yesterday, today, and forever.
He is an *everlasting* Friend. He lives forev-
er, for death has no power over Him.
He is our *soon-returning* Friend. He will soon come
again to take us to His heavenly home.

"Circumstances may separate friends; the restless waters of the wide sea may roll between us and them. But no circumstances, no distance, can separate us from the Saviour. Wherever we may be, He is at our right hand, to support, maintain, uphold, and cheer. Greater than the love of a mother for her child is Christ's love for His redeemed. It is our privilege to rest in His love, to say, 'I will trust Him; for He gave His life for me.' Human love may change, but Christ's love knows no change. When we cry to Him for help, His hand is stretched out to save."[28]

What else can be said about this Friend, except to repeat that He Who is "the Chiefest among ten thousand" and He Who is "altogether lovely" is actually "my Beloved and my Friend"? His love, which is so amazing and so divine, is also intensely personal—*my* Beloved and *my* Friend!

Oh, there's one more thing. It is the use of the word *this* to describe our Beloved and our Friend. The word is emphatic: "*This* is my Beloved, *this* is my Friend" (v. 16).

This is a grammatical word used to indicate somebody or something that has already been mentioned or identified as near, present, or available. As opposed to *that,* the word *this* gives a sense of immediacy. And in contradistinction from *these,* the word *this* emphasizes particularity—one among many.

In reference to our Lord Jesus Christ, *this* emphasizes that whereas there are other "beloveds" and "friends" in the world, Christ's love and friendship are unique. His is always available and always near. The accessibility and closeness of Christ defines the nature of true love and true friendship. Borrowing the language of one of our simple rhymed poems in chapter 2,

This Beloved and This Friend . . .

Is always there when you're sad
Makes you laugh when you're mad
And goes great lengths to make you glad

Others will break up with you. But Christ will always be there for you. He'll be there whenever you call. He'll stay with you when ills befall. And He'll help you triumph through it all.

No wonder that the greatest love story ever written points to Christ and joyously declares: "This is my Beloved, This is my Friend." It is the same Christ we present to you, dear reader, when the title of this book announces, *This Is Love.*

Christ is all we need. His love is all-sufficient, for He is the embodiment of love. The pages of sacred Scripture all point to our Lord Jesus Christ, and proclaim, "This is love!"

No love poems, love quotes, love notes, love gems, or love thoughts can adequately explicate the meaning of love. For God is love, and human words cannot fully explain Him. But wherever the spirit of this love is found, it is always known by its fruits, and it always leads a person to salvation in Christ. He is love.

I Know He's Love . . .
'Cause He'll remain my best Friend
Till life's days of toil shall end
Or to Heav'n we both ascend[29]

Notes:

1. The Bible frequently employs the analogy of bridegroom and bride to describe the relationship between God and His people. For example, the prophet Isaiah writes: "As a bridegroom rejoices over his bride, so will your God rejoice over you" (Isaiah 62:5). The Lord speaks through the prophet Hosea, when He describes how He will woo His backslidden children and marry them to Himself: "Therefore I am now going to allure her; and I will lead her into the desert and speak tenderly to her. . . . I will betroth you to Me forever; I will betroth you in righteousness and justice, in love and compassion. I will betroth you in faithfulness and you will acknowledge the Lord" (Hosea 2:14, 19, 20). In the New Testament, the marriage relationship between the groom and the bride is used to symbolize the unity of Christ with His church (see, for example, Ephesians 5:22-33).

2. In several places in the Song of Songs, the groom himself describes the bride in passionate terms. See, for example, chapter 1:15-17; 2:2; 4:1-15; 7:1-9.

3. For the summary cited here, I am indebted to the insightful sermons and/or commentaries by such Bible students as C. H. Spurgeon, Hamilton Smith, Andrew Millar, R. A. Redford, B. C. Caffin, J. D. Davies, J. R. Thomson,

S. Conway, and Tom Hayes. These commentaries are readily available in the following works: Joseph S. Exell, "The Song of Songs," in *The Biblical Illustrator*, 23 vols. (Grand Rapids: Baker, n.d.), vol. 7, pp. 110-127; "Proverbs, Ecclesiastes, Song of Solomon," vol. 9 of *The Pulpit Commentary,* ed. H. D. M. Spence and Joseph S. Exell (Peabody, Mass.: Hendrikson Publishers, n.d.), pp. 119-143; Tom Hayes, *The Unveiled Christ* (Greenville, S.C.: Ambassador–Emerald International, 2000), pp. 93-100; G. Lloyd Carr, *The Song of Solomon: An Introduction and Commentary,* The Tyndale Old Testament Commentaries, gen. ed. D.J. Wiseman (Downers Grove, Ill.: InterVarsity, 1984), pp. 139-144.

4. Read again chapter 13 of this book and reflect on the meaning of Calvary.
5. Supreme majesty may be indicated by "the most fine gold," as in Daniel 2:38.
6. Hebrews 1:3.
7. Colossians 1:18.
8. Hosea 7:9.
9. Hamilton Smith.
10. Hayes, p. 95.
11. 2 Chronicles 16:9.
12. Habakkuk 1:13.
13. Hamilton Smith.
14. Romans 3:13, 14, *New Living Translation.*
15. Isaiah 6:5.
16. John 7:46.
17. *The Desire of Ages*, p. 353.
18. Isaiah 50:4.
19. John Gill's *Exposition of the Song of Solomon* (1728), on chapter 5, verse 13.
20. E. G. White, *The Ministry of Healing,* p. 24.
21. Psalm 111:7, 8.
22. The same word rendered "belly" in Song of Songs 5:14 is used in an earlier verse (v. 4), but it is translated "bowels." In Scripture, the word translated as "belly" in Song of Songs (*me'eh*) is often translated as "bowels" and is used in a figurative or metaphorical sense to denote

the seat of emotions. For example, the prophet Jeremiah employs it a couple of times to capture God's deep compassion for His people. Thus, when mourning over the impending judgment upon Judah, God spoke through the prophet Jeremiah saying, "My *bowels*, my *bowels*! I am pained at my very heart; my heart maketh a noise in me; I cannot hold my peace, because thou hast heard, O my soul, the sound of the trumpet, the alarm of war" (Jeremiah 4:19). Again he writes: "Is Ephraim My dear son? is he a pleasant child? for since I spake against him, I do earnestly remember him still: therefore My *bowels* are troubled for him; I will surely have mercy upon him, saith the Lord" (Jeremiah 31:20). "Behold, O Lord; for I am in distress: my *bowels* are troubled; mine heart is turned within me; for I have grievously rebelled: abroad the sword bereaveth, at home there is as death" (Lamentations 1:20). "Mine eyes do fail with tears, my bowels are troubled, my liver is poured upon the earth, for the destruction of the daughter of my people; because the children and the sucklings swoon in the streets of the city" (Lamentations 2:11). Other examples are found Psalm 22:14; Isaiah 16:11, 63:15.

23. Lamentations 3:22, 23.

24. E. G. White, *Education*, p. 78.

25. E. G. White, *The Ministry of Healing*, p. 249.

26. Hayes, p. 98.

27. J. R. Thompson, *Pulpit Commentary*, p. 143.

28. E. G. White *The Ministry of Healing*, p. 72.

29. In addition to Song of Songs 5:16, the above poem was inspired by the following scriptural passages: Romans 8:35-39: "Who shall separate us from the love of Christ? Shall trouble or hardship or persecution or famine or nakedness or danger or sword? . . . No, in all these things we are more than conquerors through Him Who loved us. For I am convinced that neither death nor life, neither angels nor demons, neither the present nor the future, nor any powers, neither height nor depth, nor anything else in all creation, will be able to separate us from the love of God that is in Christ Jesus our Lord." Matthew 28:18-20: "Then Jesus came to them and said, 'All authority in heaven and on earth has been given to me. Therefore go and make disciples of all nations, baptizing them in the name of the Father and of the Son and of the Holy Spirit, and teaching them to obey everything I have commanded you. And surely I am with you always, to the very end of the age.'" 1 Thesslonians 4:16-18: "For the Lord himself will come down from heaven, with a loud command, with the voice of the archangel and with the trumpet

call of God, and the dead in Christ will rise first. After that, we who are still alive and are left will be caught up together with them in the clouds to meet the Lord in the air. And so we will be with the Lord forever. Therefore encourage each other with these words."

Recommended Reading

If *This Is Love* has been a blessing to you, you will also greatly appreciate another insightful book by the author and some life-changing works by his favorite Christian writer. These recommended books are for all those who seek solid biblical answers and authentic Christian spirituality. (Information about how to obtain them is found at the end of this section.)

Author's Book on Trials and Afflictions

Although ***Patience in the Midst of Trials and Afflictions*** is the result of the author's lifelong quest for meaningful answers to the problem of suffering and pain, the immediate impetus for this work was a series of trying events the author recently suffered. These painful experiences prepared him to reflect anew on the universal problem of suffering—grief, loss, hurt, hardships, perplexities, injustice, persecution, etc. ***Patience in the Midst of Trials and Afflictions*** insightfully explains the nature of patience, why God permits trials and afflictions, and how you can benefit from them. This life-changing book will be a source of encouragement to you and your loved ones. It will give you confidence in God's guidance and renew your determination to trust Him, no matter what. ISBN: 1-890014-04-4. Price: $10.99.

Author's Favorite Christian Writer

Although *This Is Love* contains a number of love quotes and love gems from many different authors, you may have noticed that the book makes a generous use of the spiritual insights of the nineteenth-century devotional writer, Ellen G. White (1827-1915). Millions of readers around the world have found her works to be Bible-based, faith-building, and spiritually uplifting.

Following are some of Ellen G. White's life-changing books. These best-selling Christian classics can be read online at the Ellen G. White Estate website: *http://www.WhiteEstate.org/books/books.asp.* You can also obtain printed copies at the addresses provided at the end of this section.

Steps to Christ deals with the central issue of how to become and remain a Christian—the concern at the core of Mrs. White's voluminous writing. This life-changing masterpiece on successful Christian living has been published in about 150 languages, with well over 100 million copies in circulation. It is the shortest book listed here. ISBN: 1-883012-59-7. Price: $4.98.

Patriarchs and Prophets presents the story of the conflict between good and evil—between Christ and Satan—from its beginning, starting with the origin of evil, then taking up the Creation of the world, the Bible patriarchs, Israel's Egyptian bondage and Exodus, and their establishment in Canaan up to the time of David. ISBN: 1-883012-71-6. Price: $11.99.

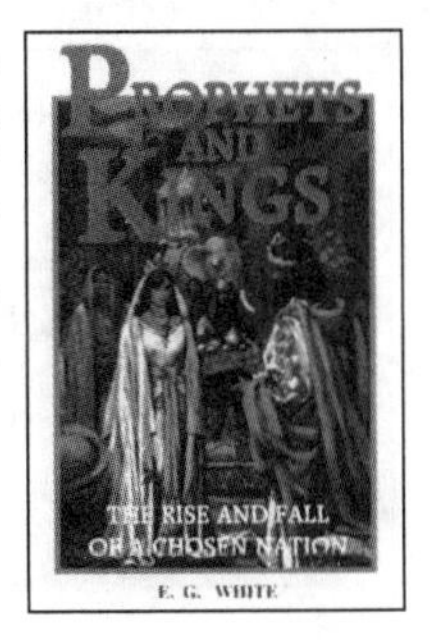

Prophets and Kings continues the story from the time of Solomon through the remaining kings of Israel and Judah and the times of the prophets, including the time of Israel's captivity and restoration, down to the first advent of Christ. ISBN: 1-883012-72-4. Price: $11.99.

The Desire of Ages is Ellen G. White's classic on the life and ministry of Jesus. Millions of readers recognize it as the best devotional work ever published on the life of Christ. ISBN: 1-883012-73-2. Price: $11.99.

Living the Life of the Lifegiver, a companion volume to *The Desire of Ages*, presents the parables of Jesus in a fresh light, showing their application to Christian living today. Also known as *Christ's Object Lessons*, this book offers a study of the key verses of Jesus' Sermon on the Mount. Included are the Beatitudes, the Lord's Prayer, and much of Jesus' other instruction for living here and now as a citizen of His kingdom. ISBN: 1-883012-67-8. Price: $9.95.

The Acts of the Apostles presents the story of the early Christian church through the rest of New Testament times. It explains what the Holy Spirit can do in the lives of ordinary people who are totally surrendered to the Lord. ISBN: 1-883012-74-0. Price: $11.99.

The Great Controversy picks up the story at the destruction of Jerusalem and follows, in broad outline, the major issues of the conflict between Christ and Satan as they have been seen in the history of the Christian church down to our own day—and beyond, based on what the Bible says will yet take place. It deals with current events in the light of Bible prophecy. Many consider this work to be the most important book they have ever read. ISBN: 1-883012-75-9. Price: $11.99.

The Ministry of Healing provides a well-rounded look at the principles of healthful living, beginning with the ministry of Jesus and extending to the life and ministry of every Christian. It covers such practical issues as vegetarian diet, exercise, peace of mind, natural remedies, prenatal influences, and health education. ISBN: 1-883012-56-2. Price: $11.95.

The Bible Study Companion Set, also known as "The Conflict of the Ages Series," is a magnificent devotional commentary on the entire Bible. The attractive set consists of five of the books listed above—*Patriarchs and Prophets, Prophets and Kings, The Desire of Ages, The Acts of the Apostles,* and *The Great Controversy.* It also includes a helpful Bible study guide. This set is an excellent resource for those who want to understand and enjoy the Bible. ISBN: 1-883012-76-7. Price: $59.95.

Available and Affordable

Many Christian Book Centers around the world can help you procure your personal copies of the author's *Patience in the Midst of Trials and Afflictions* and the above best-selling Christian classics by his favorite Christian writer. You may, however, obtain these life-changing books at the Remnant Publications website: http://www.RemnantPublications.com (click on "Devotional Classics"). Or contact:

Remnant Publications

P. O. Box 426
Coldwater, Michigan 49036, U.S.A.
Tel.: 1-800-423-1319 (toll-free)
Tel.: 1-423-279-1304
Fax: (517) 279-1804
info@remnantpublications.com
http://www.remnantpublications.com